Praise for
Feel Free to Prosper

"If you have an intense desire to live a prosperous life, this book is for you! Get two, and give one to a friend and then study this together. Marilyn Jenett shares the wisdom and understanding you need to immediately attract prosperity."

—BOB PROCTOR, world-renowned speaker and mentor,
and author of *The ABCs of Success*

"*Feel Free to Prosper* reveals the immutable, universal principles that govern prosperity. Apply them, and watch how your life becomes enriched on all levels."

—MICHAEL BERNARD BECKWITH, founder and Spiritual Director
of Agape International Spiritual Center, and author of *Life Visioning*

"During one of my most difficult times, Marilyn's Feel Free to Prosper guidance immediately shifted my perspective, and positive outcomes followed within two weeks! Reading this book, I'm reminded of Marilyn's natural grace—to instill in us our power to live the good life—starting from our subconscious mind. She makes New Age theories relevant and practical. An inspiring read I'm glad to keep in my library of favorites!"

—CATHERINE GARCEAU, Olympic medalist (Sydney 2000),
speaker, health and wellness coach, and author of *Swimming Out of Water*

"For a book on spiritual wisdom, this is a beautiful creation: well-written and inspirational."

—MARK ROBERT WALDMAN, leading neuroscientist, faculty at Loyola Marymount University, Los Angeles, and author of *Words Can Change Your Brain* and *How God Changes Your Brain* (a 2012 Oprah "Must Read")

"I adore this book! Marilyn has taken the concept of prosperity and made me believe I had the power to create it! As a healer, I know belief is everything in creating what you want. This book made me believe! Marilyn captures the excitement of knowing you can do it. Absolutely!"

—DEE WALLACE, star of *E.T. the Extra-Terrestrial*, film and television actress, healer, and author of *Bright Light*

"Marilyn delivers insightful, specific tools to empower others to achieve extraordinary success. This entertaining book synthesizes elusive information and processes to be an essential instruction manual in an evolving success story."

—DAVID KRUEGER, MD, CEO at MentorPath, and author of *The Secret Language of Money*

"'Fascinating . . .' as Mr. Spock would say. I am reading your book . . . and it is riveting! Your writings are laser-focused, easy-to-grasp, and very powerful. I'm still struck by your brevity and ability to make the complex simple. I think there is a huge, huge market hungering for that. There is a line around the globe awaiting your book release, hungry to be fed, but too impatient for a ten-course meal. They want the main course right away, presented beautifully, without any wasted calories."

—ALAN ALLARD, PH.D., speaker, corporate coach, former psychotherapist, and author of *Seven Secrets to Enlightened Happiness* and *Mental Aikido: Rediscover Your Powerful Self*

Feel Free
to Prosper

Feel Free to Prosper

Two Weeks to Unexpected Income
with the Simplest Prosperity
Laws Available

Marilyn Jenett

JEREMY P. TARCHER/PENGUIN
An imprint of Penguin Random House *New York*

JEREMY P. TARCHER/PENGUIN
An imprint of Penguin Random House LLC
375 Hudson Street
New York, New York 10014

Most Tarcher/Penguin books are available at special quantity discounts for bulk purchase for sales promotions, premiums, fund-raising, and educational needs. Special books or book excerpts also can be created to fit specific needs. For details, write: SpecialMarkets@penguinrandomhouse.com.

Library of Congress Cataloging-in-Publication Data

Jenett, Marilyn, author.
Feel free to prosper : two weeks to unexpected income with the simplest
prosperity laws available / Marilyn Jenett.
pages cm
Includes bibliographical references.
ISBN 978-0-399-17489-6
1. New Thought.   2. Success.   3. Wealth.   I. Title.
BF639.J44 2015
650.1—dc23
2015026195

Printed in the United States of America
1   3   5   7   9   10   8   6   4   2

Book design by Alissa Rose Theodor

This book is dedicated to all Feel Free to Prosper students.

I am living my life's purpose because of you.

Please, Universe, give me a sign ...

FeelFreetoProsper.com

Contents

Foreword

In this flooded book industry where there are so many books on the virtual and nonvirtual bookshelves in the area of self-help and/or prosperity, I was, I admit, extremely reluctant to agree to write the foreword for another book. However, within the first few minutes I was pleasantly surprised and, as I read on, this book maintained a deep interest all the way through, chapter by chapter.

Feel Free to Prosper is one of the most complete encyclopedias for prosperity consciousness I have ever come across.

In a matter of a few words, I would describe *Feel Free to Prosper* as the "Modern Day Neville Goddard."

For many years now I've studied, applied, experienced, written about, spoken on, and taught the principles of prosperity consciousness. There have been many teachers that have come across my path, and after reading thousands of books on the subject, purchasing and listening to thousands of audios, and attending countless programs all over the world, I have come to know the true authentic and effective books, audios, programs, and material.

The great news is that you don't have to invest years or even decades looking for the most influential and effective ideas and principles to create more abundance in your life. You need look no further than the pages of this great masterpiece.

Prosperity isn't something you "get to" . . . it is something you already are.

My recommendation to you, dear reader, is to dig into this book with great hunger and thirst. Drink from this wisdom, devour the brilliance on each of these pages, and put this into practice. I'm quite certain your world will change *only* for the better.

As Marilyn suggests in Chapter 14: "Once you have instilled in your deeper mind the idea of what you wish to attract, you must be able to let go of the *How* in order to manifest and enjoy the *Wow.*"

Could it be that having what you deeply desire is as simple as that?

Read on and you'll be pleasantly surprised by how simple manifestation really is when you are given these solid ideas.

I myself enjoy a fulfilling and prosperous life. I'm grateful to Marilyn for having written this book, as I envision you also enjoying a totally fulfilling life. You certainly deserve it. May you be blessed with an abundance of all good things.

—PEGGY MCCOLL, *New York Times* bestselling author and book marketing expert known as *"The Best Seller Maker"*

Introduction

The Promise

Two weeks to achieve unexpected income, unexpected business, unexpected supply in all areas of life. This is the promise of *Feel Free to Prosper: Two Weeks to Unexpected Income with the Simplest Prosperity Laws Available*, a simple, fast, and practical how-to approach to prosperity. And it is not a promise made lightly. It's a bold promise I make to you—and one that I intend to keep.

It's not magic. But it may seem magical because the exquisite simplicity of the prosperity laws is not commonly understood. Human nature tends to complicate matters that appear abstract and beyond our reach.

I overcame my own severe "lack" consciousness to create a business that, for two decades, attracted the world's largest corporate clients by using the same prosperity principles that I now share with my students internationally and that I am about to share with you. Marilyn Jenett Locations, my one-woman special event company, evolved and was sustained over the years solely through the application of these prosperity laws and what I refer to as "synchronicity and guidance." With the wisdom gained from my experiences in life and business, and through the inspired intuition that created this material, I am passionate about teaching you how to "have the Universe on speed dial" through my amazingly simple, easy-to-grasp, and practical Feel Free to Prosper teachings.

There is a vital need for the world's population to understand the underlying cause of personal financial distress: a belief that there is a separation from the true source of their supply—what I call our "invisible means of support." With my teachings, you will finally overcome the fear and experience proof of your alignment with the universal parent that is ready to shower each of us with gifts that are far beyond our imaginings—once we learn how to receive.

The book you are about to read was never intended to be a book. The content was written online over several years in my characteristic conversational tone. Its purpose was to inspire my students and followers with the knowledge I had acquired while applying the works of the most brilliant teachers of mental and spiritual laws, starting almost forty years ago. My own teaching methods and proprietary techniques allow you to bypass the analytical mind and gently influence the subconscious, thereby connecting with the ultimate and unlimited source of abundant supply and knowledge. I am constantly told that my unique teaching style and ability to communicate what was previously considered esoteric knowledge into the simplest ideas is the key to the successful results my students achieve.

Why two weeks? From my decades of study of the mind, I knew that it was commonly accepted that it took three to four weeks to break a habit and create a new mental pattern. However, from the time I began teaching my Feel Free to Prosper program, I noticed that my average student achieved a breakthrough in two weeks—often much sooner. I later heard that current psychological research showed it could take as little as two weeks to begin creating a new neural pathway in the brain. My students have been consistently right on cue. Quite simply, the techniques work, and they work fast.

The fulfillment of my promise and your two-week adventure will officially launch when you apply the legendary Feel Free to Prosper lesson material at the end of this book. But the chapters leading up to that program will not only jump-start your prosperity—they will prepare you well for the main ride. Feel Free to Prosper is not a band-aid. It's a cure.

Feel Free to Prosper is by no means intended to be just a typical tutorial or "how-to" book. My loftiest aspiration is to connect with you, my reader, in an uncommon way. I wish to instill in you my own faith and conviction in these laws, making you feel mentally—even spiritually—"at home," inspiring you to embrace and apply the nuggets in each lesson for your happiness and success.

Common Ground

Many of the books on the market today are designed to establish expertise and attract readers to high-priced seminars and products. I don't find anything wrong with that. However, I have a special place in my heart for the millions of people for whom such offerings are out of reach. I recall this quote by Abraham Lincoln: "God must have loved the common man because he made so many of them."

In my heart, I consider myself the "common man's prosperity teacher," although successful professionals are equally at home with my material. My student base consists largely of entrepreneurs, "solo-preneurs," and businesspeople, but my special mission is to help those whose "containers" (consciousness) are not yet large enough for pricey offerings. They are most urgently reaching out for answers and can benefit profoundly from the right book, as I—a common woman—once did.

The Teachings and the Gift

This book is organized into several primary parts. The chapters within each section contain material that I have written spontaneously—and intuitively—for my students and followers since creating Feel Free to Prosper. Little did I know that the Universe was actually dictating the chapters for my future book. Later in the book, inspiring stories in my students' own words provide a testament to the power of these teachings and the universal laws.

The chapters within each part are not necessarily in an order meant to be followed sequentially, so you may refer to them for reinforcement or review at any time based on the subject and title.

You'll find in a few instances that I've repeated certain wording in different chapters. That's because those items pertain to each of those chapters. Additionally, the repetition will help your subconscious mind accept these important points.

You may notice that I don't emphasize the term "law of attraction" and other buzzwords that have become mainstream in recent years. That's because my studies of the laws spanned several decades and I created Feel Free to Prosper several years before those concepts became popular. With due respect to the modern wave of teachers, I want the world to remember those brilliant icons who came before us—the legendary teachers who influenced me the most and whose legacy I now wish to honor.

While the main subject of this book is learning how to achieve financial prosperity, you will find that the principles can be easily adapted to other areas of your life. The teachings in Part One provide the perfect foundation to apply the universal laws and prosperity principles for any purpose.

The knowledge and wisdom shared throughout this book culminate in my final gift that will fulfill my promise: I am including my **Feel Free to Prosper program lesson that relates to my "two-week" promise**, along with access to the recording of the companion group mentoring session. This is the proprietary lesson material that has resulted in strikingly fast results for my students. When you apply the program, it's important to follow my lesson instructions exactly and in the sequence presented for your greatest results. You will be firmly grounded on your path to prosperity and will experience the exhilaration of finally achieving the key to manifesting—both the expected and unexpected.

Testimonials from the Feel Free to Prosper program come from men and women from all walks of life across the globe. You will be joining my students, who include business owners and employees, entrepreneurs, working moms, sales agents, professionals, job seekers, coaches, healers, retirees, artists, entertainers, and even an Olympic champion.

Overcoming the Resistance of the Subconscious Mind

There is a multitude of self-help and get-rich material in the marketplace available to those interested in improving their lives and increasing their prosperity. People bounce from one book or program to the next looking for results, but instead they often meet with frustration because the "law of attraction" tools being touted simply don't offer enough.

My students get the results they are looking for—and get them quickly—because my teachings address a critical component and missing link that most other books and programs do not: overcoming the resistance of the subconscious mind.

The reason most people, even those who are well versed in attraction and prosperity laws, do not manifest easily comes down to the resistance of the subconscious mind. If your subconscious mindset is not in alignment with your conscious desires, and you use law-of-attraction-type techniques to try and achieve life changes, you will automatically revert back to the tangible evidence of your own core beliefs. And it is those subconscious core beliefs which keep you stuck in "lack" rather than prosperity, whether we are talking about income, health, or abundance in any other forms.

Through what I call "friendly persuasion," my Feel Free to Prosper students learn—and now you will learn—to use my special techniques and the power of words to persuade rather than argue with the subconscious. In *Feel Free to Prosper* and the included lesson program, you'll learn specific techniques that gently coerce the subconscious mind to accept a new dominant thought. This shift in thinking then creates the fertile soil of the subconscious which allows the new ideas of wealth, health, abundance, and success to take root. Most importantly, the Feel Free to Prosper techniques will bridge the gap between having an intellectual grasp of the prosperity principles—which many people do, but to no avail—and instilling a subconscious acceptance of them.

Advertisers have known for a long time that the subconscious mind responds to ideas that are simple and to the point. *Feel Free to Prosper* teaches these universal laws and prosperity principles in the simplest practical terms, thereby inspiring and guiding you toward the success you desire.

The Universe—Your Marketing Department

If you own a business or want to advance in your job or career, then an entire section of this book is devoted to you.

Just as a house cannot stand without a proper foundation, all of the marketing, sales, and business know-how in the world will not result in success unless you first have the internal foundation—the mindset—to succeed. Once you create that foundation, you will automatically be guided to all the appropriate elements that will result in your success. You will be guided to do exactly what needs to be done to get your results. Or you may be guided to take no physical action—except to watch as results arrive miraculously out of the blue. (I know you'll love that part of these teachings.)

As a reader of *Feel Free to Prosper*, you will learn that when you "put the Universe on speed dial" you will truly have the greatest marketing department you could ever hope for—and that the possibilities are unlimited.

There is no question in my mind that the use of prosperity principles—based on mental and spiritual laws—is by far the most valuable way to market your business, achieve ongoing success in your business or career, and achieve success in every aspect of life. You can "prosper" in finances, in health, in love and relationships, in creativity and spiritually. As my greatest teacher, Dr. Joseph Murphy, used to say and that I now tell my students, "Do the homework and you'll get the results."

Synchronicity and Guidance

Achieving prosperity is not just about visualizing and attracting what you want, as many books and programs would have you believe. By gently coercing the subconscious to accept the new dominant thought, we are able to create our "pipeline" to and tap into the universal source of supply—and spontaneously attract and be guided to results which are far beyond what our limited, finite minds can imagine or visualize. My journey of successfully using these teachings to become the constant recipient of striking and unexpected gifts from this universal source is well documented in my manuscript *Feel Free to Prosper: An Entrepreneurial Memoir of Synchronicity and Guidance.* The memoir was written entirely online on my former social media forum and attracted tens of thousands of views. Then came literary agents and book offers based on my teachings, which ultimately led to my publisher and the book you are reading.

Early in my career as a special event specialist, with no PR or marketing resources and using only my prosperity principles and the "universe as my publicist," I manifested a cover feature story in the *Los Angeles Times* that attracted thousands of telephone calls for years and syndication around the world. This was followed by local and national prime-time television segments and continuing media exposure, including the first article I ever wrote that grossed $250,000 for my business!

During the next two decades, my tiny one-woman company continued to spontaneously attract many of the world's largest corporate clients—without marketing, advertising, networking, or cold calling. But there were also severe setbacks related to local disasters and national recessions, and those experiences were my greatest learning experiences—they taught me what worked and what didn't. I realize now that my entrepreneurial journey and my business served as the "schoolhouse" where I became indoctrinated in the most profound laws of the Universe. My victory in overcoming my own "lack" consciousness culminated in my faith and conviction in these laws and the recognition of my life's purpose—and spiritual obligation—to teach others.

Today I continue to use the prosperity laws to maintain the mindset to attract success. Despite the fact that I released my corporate business years ago to devote myself to teaching Feel Free to Prosper, I still spontaneously attracted huge corporate clients—even at the height of the 2008 recession, considered the worst since the 1930s—while I was advocating "progression, not recession" in my writings and interviews. I accepted a couple of bookings because I felt that the Universe sent them to publicly support my conviction that, with the right mindset, we can prosper in any economy. But following those bookings, I made the decision that I would never coordinate another event. I knew that my life had transitioned permanently and there was no turning back. My heart and soul would be exclusively devoted to helping others with my teachings.

A month after I made that decision, I was offered the first of what eventually turned out to be three publishing offers to write this book.

So you see, I consistently rely on the same universal laws and principles that I teach my students and I am perpetually in awe of the synchronicity and guidance that will govern our lives once we become aligned to our source.

Now It's Your Turn

You are here because you are ready to move beyond your present circumstances and fulfill the potential that you know deep in your heart is within you. You may be a beginner who yearns to break through a lifetime of struggle to the blissful state of knowing your financial needs are always met. Or maybe you have reached a certain level of accomplishment but have not been able to advance further. Perhaps your greatest desire is for direction—to have your true place in life revealed so that you can profit financially from work that you truly love and were born to do. You may even be a seasoned seeker with knowledge of the laws but find something is missing that prevents you from translating your knowledge into practical results. In *Feel Free to Prosper*, I promise that I will simply and passionately share my experiences and knowledge with you so that you can live a more prosperous, inspiring, and successful life.

Part One

~~~~~

Cosmic Relief—
An Introduction to Universal Laws
and Prosperity Principles

The trouble with most people is that they have no invisible
means of support.

—DR. JOSEPH MURPHY

Part One is the perfect introduction that will enhance your understanding of the mental and spiritual laws and the prosperity principles that are the foundation of the Feel Free to Prosper program and teachings. It will raise your awareness and start you on your journey to grow a prosperity consciousness.

I'm known for my practical, down-to-earth teachings that make these abstract concepts easy to understand so that you can readily apply them to make striking changes in your life. If you have seen the movie *The Secret*, but crave more specific information to apply the law of attraction in your life, this material will provide it. But it will also introduce you to other, equally important laws and valuable principles that will speed your progress.

This section allows you to learn powerful prosperity principles that you can apply immediately. It tills the soil of your subconscious mind to prepare for the planting of seeds in the specific areas of life presented in later sections and chapters.

Included with the practical wisdom, prosperity techniques, and inspiration contained in this section, you will learn:

- The basis of mental and spiritual principles.

- Why affirmations may not be bringing you results.

- Why you don't have to "strive" or try to create success. In fact, you will learn why trying will never get you there.

- Why your business, job, clients, customers, or investments are *not* your source of income.

- How to open your pipeline and create the connection to your true source of supply.

- The words that you are habitually using that are preventing your success.

- How to handle setbacks—and my personal concept of staying in "neutral."

- An aspect of gratitude that is not commonly known and that can change your circumstances dramatically, often at an astounding speed.

- How Professor Higgins and Eliza Doolittle revealed a key to manifestation decades before *The Secret*.

- You don't attract what you want, you attract what you are.

And so much more . . .

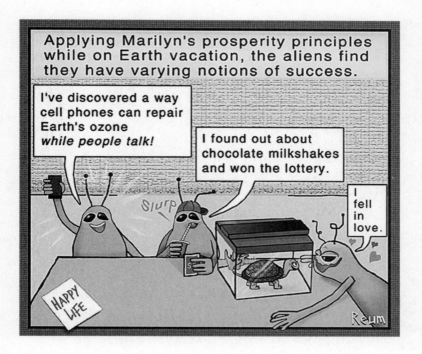

1

So, What *Are* These Mental and Spiritual Laws?

In this chapter I am first going to give you a basic introduction to universal laws that will lead to your understanding of prosperity principles. Then I am going to share my knowledge of how the principles work when we align ourselves with them. By using the principles I teach, you can magnetize your good to you and turn your negative situations around dramatically.

The Universe

The Universe as we know it, see it, and experience it is not all there is. The Universe is always in motion—it is a vibrating, pulsating, resonating, magnetizing force, and at the molecular level everything is in motion. It is pure energy.

What we are talking about here is the pure, formless substance of the Universe. We can think of this in spiritual terms as God, Higher Power, Spirit, or the Universe, or we can address it mentally as Infinite Intelligence, Universal Mind, Divine Mind, or Formless Substance. We can also think of it scientifically as Energy or Relativity, or we can take a giant leap into the area of quantum physics, where this pure, formless substance is known as the Field of All Possibilities.

What a great age of discovery we live in! The mental, the spiritual, the scientific aspect of the laws of life—any or all of it is there for the asking. However you perceive it, this Power is the source of everything we desire. It is awaiting our recognition and will create, attract, and guide us to inspired action. It will magnetize and mold itself to whatever form we desire if we align ourselves with it through certain laws—called universal laws.

The Laws

What are these laws? Well, we know that there are laws of physics, laws of chemistry, laws of mathematics. But most people are not aware of the laws that govern the mental and spiritual realms—the creative laws of the Universe that govern our existence. Or you may know something about them but don't know how to relate to them or how to use them.

So how do we know these laws exist or even that this Universe or Power exists—aside from any intuitive feeling that it does or because Marilyn says it does? We know because of its *responsiveness*. We know by the results we experience when we align ourselves with it. And I can tell you from my own personal experience that once you become aware of the response of this Universal Presence, you will never be the same. You will feel a love and a connectedness and a sense of security that is greater than anything you have felt on an earthly level.

The laws work for everyone alike. The law of gravity works for everyone, doesn't it? Successful people are using the mental and spiritual laws—they just may not realize they are doing so. And guess what? You are using these laws all of the time whether *you* realize it or not. Only you are most likely not using them for the purpose and intention that you consciously desire. How many things have you attracted into your life that you feel you did nothing to deserve and asked, "Why did this happen?"

Remember I said that the universal laws are simple? The actual principles and techniques that relate to the laws are also surprisingly simple. Well, let's use the law of gravity as an example. We do not need to have a vast knowledge of the laws of physics to understand how gravity works. We know that if we step off a tall building, we will fall.

We know that if we align ourselves with this law correctly, we won't have any mishaps, right? It is exactly the same with the mental and spiritual laws. If we align ourselves with them correctly, we won't have mishaps. We will instead experience joyful results.

So how do we align ourselves with these laws? We connect with this Power, this creative force of the Universe, within, through the channel of our subconscious minds—through our thoughts and our feelings. The subconscious mind is the most fantastic computer you could ever imagine. It keeps our heart beating, our lungs breathing, and has perfect memory of every cell in our body. It has also recorded and stored everything that we have ever heard, said, felt, and experienced. Unfortunately, that includes all of the faulty beliefs and negative patterns from others that we have acquired from the time we were very young through our entire lifetime.

Our thoughts, our feelings, our deepest beliefs are the key to

connecting with the Power that responds to our desires. But first
we must break through and overcome the negative thought patterns and beliefs that we have acquired since childhood. We cannot delete anything from the subconscious mind, and it is not
necessary to do so. In order to shift our consciousness, we simply
create a new *dominant thought*.

Dominant Thought

The subconscious mind does not like to change and will create
resistance. (We know that from our attempts to change a habit.)
But there are techniques and methods for influencing the subconscious in a way that does not create argument. I call this "friendly
persuasion." We *gently* shift the consciousness to create a new
dominant thought in the mind.

That is the key. The *dominant* thought.

The dominant thought in our conscious and our subconscious
is what determines our circumstances. Why do we attract those
things that we don't desire? Those results are the outcropping of
the thoughts and impressions that are established in the mind
subconsciously. So we must shift our consciousness to a new dominant thought—a new awareness. When we do so, we then open
ourselves to the influence of the creative power of the Universe, to
what I call our "invisible means of support."

The subconscious records everything—everything that you
have ever heard or said or felt is recorded in perfect memory,
whether you were conscious of it or not. And often the more casual
words you use are the ones that drop into the subconscious more
easily and are accepted, because you are not monitoring them
or refuting them.

Marriage of the Conscious and Subconscious Minds

Here is an analogy that my students love with regard to manifesting our desires by creating agreement between the conscious and subconscious minds. Now, this is a very important point that I want you to remember: In order to manifest our desire, the conscious and subconscious minds must *agree* on the idea.

Think of the conscious mind as the husband, the assertive male aspect of mind. The subconscious is the wife, the receptive, female aspect. The husband impregnates the wife and when the subconscious becomes impregnated with the new seed thought—the new idea—then from this union, children are born. These children are your answered prayers, your desired results, your goals fulfilled.

It is through this marriage of the conscious and subconscious minds—when they **both** agree on an idea—that the idea will become manifest.

So we must now teach the husband how to impregnate the wife!

We make a decision with our conscious mind. We use our conscious mind to instill this idea into the subconscious until it is accepted. Once the seed has been accepted in the soil of mind, it will grow and manifest just as the seed planted in the ground will become a plant or a flower. First, we do our job and plant the seed. We nurture the soil with positive thoughts and expectation. Then we turn the job over to Universal Mind—to the creative forces. We can relax and let go. Our manifestation will come. There is no such thing as "half pregnant." Our baby will be born.

Now, from this foundation I've given you, I would like you to contemplate the message within my words. I want you to come to a clear understanding that you do not carry the burden of manifestation on your shoulders. You have at your disposal the creative forces of the entire Universe waiting to do your bidding, if you will just do your part to apply the "rules."

The only thing that is important is to learn how the system works. **And use it.** Someone once asked Henry Ford what electricity was. He answered, "Madam, it just is . . . use it."

2

By George, She's Got It!

In the legendary Broadway play, and then hit movie, *My Fair Lady*, Professor Higgins (played by the amazing Rex Harrison) took on a bet that he could turn the scruffy, foulmouthed, uneducated street urchin Eliza Doolittle (played by the equally amazing Audrey Hepburn) into a real lady.

There was the cleanup, the wardrobe, etiquette, and posture lessons, all of the exterior changes necessary for Eliza to look like a lady.

But it wasn't until Eliza learned to change her words that she became the lady. A change in her words (and how she pronounced them) produced a change in her thoughts, then a change in her consciousness, and before long Eliza was a true lady.

The words merely voiced and memorized did not do the trick. At first she committed the words to memory, but it was when those words were repeated over and over that they were accepted in consciousness. It was then that Eliza's subconscious mind took over, produced the feeling, and made her into the lady that was potentially within her, but had never manifested before Professor Higgins showed her the way.

During Eliza's practice work, the professor made her repeat

over and over, "The rain in Spain falls mainly on the plain," until her diction was correct. And finally, after exhaustive practice, Eliza said it correctly and the professor announced, "By George, she's got it!"

Eliza learned that to become a real lady, she had to talk and think like a lady.

I was reminded of this story and inspired to write this lesson from a conversation one evening with one of my students.

In almost every conversation with new students before they begin my lessons, I notice certain words that they tend to repeat, almost unconsciously. These are negative words that I notice as they are speaking, and often when I make the student aware of this, they comment that they don't even realize they are saying the words or how often they repeat them.

One student's word may be "doubt" or "doubted." With another, it might be "stress" or "stressed." The words are spoken habitually, with no real thought behind them. These are common, everyday words, but they are words that are not conducive to prosperity thinking—words that only serve to create the very things we do not want and negate the prosperity work we are doing.

A close friend's "word" was interesting to me. She was divorced after raising a family and being absent from the working world for twenty years. While giving thought to what she wanted to do as a career, opportunities arose where she was able to help friends in their businesses on a temporary basis. My friend would call and tell me that she was helping out so-and-so at their business, and she would casually state that this was keeping her busy and she was "making a little money." I realized that every time my friend mentioned the word "money," she attached the word "little" to it. When I told her about this, she seemed stunned. She was completely unaware that she was saying that word. When she eliminated the phrase, she was well on her way to increased income.

I tell every student that they must eliminate these negative words from their vocabulary, especially at the beginning during the delicate stage of shifting the subconscious thought patterns. It is necessary to break the habit of mindlessly and casually repeating these words because, as I stated earlier, it's often the words in casual conversation that drop easily into the subconscious mind and are accepted.

Once the habit is broken, the positive words and affirmations that you are applying will have the opportunity to take hold and become substance in the mind. If you continue to casually repeat negative words, then, in essence, you are denying what you affirm and giving your mind two directions, which, you will learn, will get you to no destination or the wrong one.

You must saturate your speech and thoughts with the idea of what you want, and by doing so the idea will drop into the subconscious and take permanent residence.

That is why I have labeled these words "delete" words. You must delete them from your vocabulary and make them history.

Now, Will You Get It?

The foundation of the Feel Free to Prosper teachings is the powerful impact that our words—thought and spoken, and especially written—have on our subconscious mind and Universal Mind.

Words have more power than you realize. Our words create vibratory equivalents and produce corresponding circumstances in our lives.

We manifest according to the dominant words and thoughts in our subconscious mind. Repetition imprints our words in the subconscious. Writing words has an even more powerful effect and stakes our "claim" on the Universal Mind Substance, which will return our words to us in correlating physical circumstances.

The subconscious mind does not reason or know what you are intending. It merely accepts your words as a suggestion and thinks that is what you want. So you must learn to monitor your language and eliminate those words that will sooner or later come back to haunt and do their damage.

One of the reasons that my students get such incredibly fast results is that I have them eliminate culprit words from their vocabulary entirely.

So always remember that your words are tremendously powerful. And don't forget the words you write. The subconscious mind responds to repetition, so any words that you say or write or view over and over will impact your mind. But, on the other hand, as mentioned, often our most casual words will drop into the subconscious and produce results.

The Subconscious Cannot Take a Joke

That's right. The subconscious mind accepts our words literally. Again, it does not reason or think. Therefore, the subconscious mind cannot take a joke. I am certainly not saying we shouldn't have a sense of humor. But the creative quality of that humor puts a lot at stake and we should pay attention.

And I'm really not referring to actual "ha ha" jokes as much as I am to the words that you use in everyday life.

But here's a joke to illustrate . . .

There was a man who had the good fortune to be visited by a genie. The genie told him that she would grant him three wishes only. So he was to think this over carefully before making his decision.

For his first wish, the man asked the genie to make him thirty years younger. Poof! The genie granted his wish, and the man was thrilled to find that he was young again.

The man's second wish was for a brand-new convertible sports car. (Well, what else did you expect a young man to ask for?) And poof! Suddenly he found himself driving a beautiful sleek and shiny new sports car.

Now the genie told the man to take his time and give much thought to his third and final wish.

So he was driving along the coastal highway with the top down, singing along with the radio, when a commercial came on and he continued to sing . . .

"I wish I were an Oscar Mayer wiener . . ."

Words About Others

Did you know that the subconscious mind does not know anyone else but **you**? (I'll bet you didn't.) It has no conception of consciousness other than your own. I explain to students that when we criticize others or find fault, our mind thinks we are speaking about ourselves. That's why it's so important to become aware of the power of our words, because often our words and feelings that are directed outwardly can rebound and cause havoc in our own lives.

Of course, we do these things unconsciously. The majority of people do not realize that our thoughts and words are influencing and imprinting our own minds.

So let's say we are speaking about someone who "irritates" us. And the subconscious, which does not reason or think, just interprets our words as an "order." So we share a thought about things that irritate us. And what does the subconscious hear?

Irritate.

So now it thinks we want to be irritated. And, lo and behold, some outer circumstance occurs that is sure to irritate us—more so if we are already on that frequency to begin with.

And this is even more interesting. The subconscious mind only hears the **dominant** words, not the lesser words. Even if we said something like, "She no longer irritates me," the mind doesn't hear "no longer"—it only hears "irritates me." And voilà, gremlins show up to irritate us.

Our individual thoughts and words reach into the ethers and cause the creative forces of Universal Mind to bring all the elements together to manifest what the mind thinks we want: to be irritated.

How can we stop perpetuating situations that result from these outer "triggers"? The way to stop the cycle is to no longer be influenced by what happens. I like to call this "staying in neutral." When an issue ceases to bother or affect us, the issue will then have no more energy to feed it, so it will quietly disappear. That is how to create a solution to **anything** in life. When we cease to fuel it with negative thought or energy, the situation will resolve itself or the solution will appear. But that's another complete prosperity lesson in itself—for another chapter.

3

Affirmations—Why You May Not Get Results

My students do not learn about affirmations in the beginning of the Feel Free to Prosper program. The first lesson does include two affirmations that I have specifically composed to speed the learning process and the results, but there is no detailed study of affirmations and the students do not compose their own affirmations. Later, in the second lesson, there is much to learn about the different types of affirmations—how to compose them, how to use them, when to use them, and why they may not bring results.

My knowledge about affirmations is based on decades of study of the subtleties of the subconscious mind, taught by some of the most brilliant minds in the area of mental and spiritual science and clinical hypnosis. Many of these subtleties are not addressed by today's modern teachers.

I was fortunate enough to be drawn to specific knowledge that allows us to bypass our analytical mind and influence the subconscious through what I have labeled "friendly persuasion"—specific techniques that do not create resistance in the subconscious and allow it to accept the new idea of wealth and abundance. These techniques bridge the gap between belief in the principles and subconscious acceptance of them.

Resistance

It is my intuitive guess that 80 percent or more of the people who use affirmations don't get results. That's because they are not aware of those important nuances of the mind that would allow them to overcome its resistance. Let me explain what I mean by resistance . . .

Let's say your subconscious mind has an established pattern of *lack*. You might apply the type of present-tense affirmations that are generally recommended, such as "I am wealthy" or "I am prosperous."

Do you know what happens? Your subconscious mind does not accept this and knows you are lying, your entire being feels like you are lying, you look around at appearances and you say, "Yeah, right. Who am I kidding?" So now what are you thinking about? What are you focused on? **You are now focused more on lack!** And because you are now focused on lack, your undesirable circumstances will continue to exist or may even get worse. This reminds me of "Don't think of a white elephant!"

You have learned that the subconscious mind does not like change. That part of the mind does not reason—it just accepts input as an order. Once it accepts a thought pattern, it will resist any effort to change it. So the answer lies in *not creating an argument or resistance in the subconscious*. Remember what we discussed about the *agreement* of the conscious and subconscious minds? The key to heaven is to create that agreement.

In Lesson One of Feel Free to Prosper, you will learn techniques that **gently** coerce the subconscious to accept the new prosperous idea. You will use "friendly persuasion" to create the shift without creating resistance. The affirmations in the lesson are worded specifically to till the soil of the subconscious and prepare it for the planting and acceptance of more specific prosperity seed thoughts.

Mental Gardening

Once the subconscious is prepared, it will accept the seeds that you plant. Otherwise, it will not. That is why we don't study about affirmations until later in the program. By that time, you have learned other powerful techniques to prepare your mind to accept your personal affirmations and you will learn to compose them in a way that will produce the results you want. You have done your mental gardening.

You should be aware that affirmations are not one breed. There are many types of affirmations and different ways to use them. As I mentioned, if you don't use them correctly, you may very well create the *opposite* of what you want. Even the way you were raised—whether you accepted parental authority or not as a child—may determine whether certain types of affirmations will work for you, and whether your subconscious will accept affirmations worded grammatically in the first person ("I") or second person ("you"). It's a fascinating study.

I truly believe that much of the success of the Feel Free to Prosper program has been based on these missing links to affirmative suggestion and the manifestation process.

So, you have learned that your subconscious mind cannot take a joke and that it will resist any change that you wish to make, even for the better. The good news—actually, the fabulous news—is that there are ways to make your subconscious mind your best friend so that it will support you and help you—even compel you—to create what you want. Knowledge is indeed power.

4

⌒

Source vs. Channels

Now I am going to share a very important component of my teachings. It is one of the most valuable lessons, and if you will grasp this, it can change your financial life. And it can change your entire life if you broaden your understanding beyond the monetary aspect. Here it is:

Your business is not your source of income. Your business, job, customers, clients, investments, spouse—none of these are your source of income. There is only one source of income: the Universe, God, Divine Presence, Infinite Spirit, Formless Substance (whatever your concept is of that universal source of good). The Universe is your source of supply.

That is the only source of your supply. All of those other avenues are **channels** for your supply. But they are not the source. When you truly understand and know this, then you will open the pipeline to the unlimited channels of supply that exist for you. And there are indeed unlimited channels through which your good can come to you, the unexpected along with your expected channels. But you can only become open and receptive to these free-flowing channels when you put your complete reliance on the true source.

Let's use the analogy of a kitchen faucet. The faucet is not the source of water. It is only a channel. If that channel is broken or closed, then there are an infinite number of other channels through which we can get our water.

A personal example: For two decades I was the owner of a renowned special event company servicing the corporate and convention markets. The aftermath of September 11, 2001, had a tremendous impact on our industry, as it did on many others. I was initially affected by mass mind thinking. But then a wonderful teacher arrived at just the right time and reminded me that I had to focus on Truth principles and know that my business of twenty years was not my source of supply. Of course . . . I knew what I had to do. And when I did it, channels began to open in completely unexpected areas, some totally unrelated to my regular business, and money flowed in. The Universe took care of me and provided for me. My business later rebounded beyond my dreams in ways that allowed me to fulfill my life by discovering and following my heart path—and my true purpose—the work I am doing now.

When you look to your true source of supply, it will become the Senior Partner in your business and your life, and you will prosper. You will be in your right place, in your present situation or a better one. You will be at peace. Obviously, there are other lessons to learn to speed our journey on the path to prosperity, but I cannot emphasize enough how important this one is.

5

Use the Powerful Principle of Gratitude to Attract What You Don't Yet Have

We are now going to focus on an aspect of gratitude that is not commonly known—using the powerful principle of gratitude to attract what you don't already have.

Gratitude: Thankfulness.

Thankful: Conscious of benefit received or for what we are about to receive; expressive of thanks; well pleased.

The *attitude of gratitude* is one of the greatest—perhaps *the* greatest spiritual principle that can be applied to attain happiness, inner peace, health, and financial prosperity. It is easy to be grateful for what you already have. But can you be grateful for what you don't yet see?

> *Now faith is the substance of things hoped for, the evidence of things not seen.*
>
> —HEBREWS 11:1

We are going to discuss how gratitude is your precursor to the evidence of "things not seen" and how you can acquire gratitude when there are appearances to the contrary. If you apply this uncommon aspect of gratitude, it will change your circumstances dramatically, often at an astounding speed.

Gratitude for What You Don't Have?

Gratitude is surely one of the greatest prosperity principles that can be applied to every part of our lives. But I'm not just referring to the philosophical aspect of gratitude. I'm going to address gratitude from a practical standpoint. I am going to help you understand the relationship of gratitude to "affirmative prayer," which is actually scientific prayer, and I will explain why.

We all know how to feel grateful for the blessings we have in life. But I want to teach you how you can feel grateful for those things you don't have and don't see yet and, as a result, draw them to you. How can you acquire gratitude when there are appearances to the contrary? You're about to learn how.

If you can't be thankful for what you receive, be thankful for what you escape.

—ANONYMOUS

Gratitude as the Magnet

The subconscious mind will create for us and attract to us those circumstances that it accepts to be true in the present moment. That is its nature. Its nature is compulsive. Our job is to condition our subconscious mind to accept what we want as if it's an existing reality. Tomorrow never comes. It is always the present moment or now in consciousness. When what we call later or tomorrow arrives, it will actually still be the present moment. It is always

now. And what we are thinking and feeling **now** is what determines our future, its outcomes and experiences. We create that future right this moment.

Let me ask you this . . . If you were in possession of your desired good, what else would you feel besides your joy or security in having what you want? If suddenly you experienced a windfall or found the right job or finally had that new car, or were free of your physical ailment, what emotion would fill your consciousness?

Gratitude.

If the subconscious responds to and acts upon what we feel in the present moment, then in order to feel like we already have what we want, what feeling would we need to create?

Gratitude.

By giving thanks, we acknowledge that we are receiving our good now or that we have already received it and we are grateful. To create this feeling of being grateful, we use gratitude in our words and affirmations. We are expressing our feeling of gratitude for the good that we have already received, even before we actually receive it. We think of it as—and feel it to be—an accomplished fact. We are grateful.

In other words, our gratitude is not contingent upon any tangible proof to our senses (outer conditions). Our gratitude is based only on our faith, not on conditions. That is unconditional gratitude.

Gratitude is one of the surest ways to bring your desires into the present moment. It is the magnet that reaches out into Universal Mind and pulls our good to us. It is our bridge between our desire and its manifestation. Gratitude is the umbilical cord that connects us to our universal parent. If you will replace any doubtful thoughts or begging prayers with a heart full of gratitude, you will be thrilled at how fast you'll learn to manifest your desires.

Gratitude Attracts More

An attitude of gratitude and the appreciation for the gifts we receive from the Universe open the channels for more good to be received. The more gratitude we feel, the more we attract to be grateful for. What we focus on increases and expands. The more we complain, the more we will attract to complain about. The more we express our gratitude, the more we are giving our subconscious mind and Universal Mind the message that we have much to be grateful for, and we keep attracting more.

> *What if you gave someone a gift, and they neglected to thank you for it—would you be likely to give them another? Life is the same way. In order to attract more of the blessings that life has to offer, you must truly appreciate what you already have.*
>
> —RALPH MARSTON*

The Gratitude Call and Jim

One year for Thanksgiving, I conducted a holiday teleseminar on gratitude. Everyone lost track of time as we discussed mental and spiritual laws and their relationship to the principle of gratitude.

As preparation and to create the mood for this gratitude call, I asked each participant to follow the requests that I would like you to do right now.

First, take a few moments to quietly contemplate and make a list of ten things in your life for which you feel grateful. Stop reading and do that now.

---

* Ralph Marston, The Daily Motivator, www.greatday.com.

Next, think of one or two things in your life for which you are *not* grateful at the moment. A challenge, issue, or condition that you would like to change or something missing that you would like to create. You are going to practice using gratitude as a powerful force for turning those situations around.

I had also sent a photo to the students prior to our call that I will describe . . .

I had received the photo of a man that was included in a mailed request for donations for DAV (Disabled American Veterans). I was so taken and inspired by Jim's picture that I had to save it.

It brought so much into perspective when I realized how easy it was to complain about things in our lives, when in reality we have so much to be grateful for.

Jim was a handsome man dressed in a jacket and tie and smiling from his wheelchair. But he had only one arm and no legs. Jim wasn't born this way. He lost three limbs in Vietnam. His note which was attached to the photo stated in part:

"I thought I lost everything in Vietnam, but thanks to the DAV, my life was turned around . . ."

If this man can turn his life around, find his peace, and express gratitude for what he has in life, then shouldn't it be that much easier for us to take our gratitude consciousness to another level?

After thinking about Jim, please make another list of *ten more* things you have in life for which to be grateful.

During the call, I also shared the story about when I was held up at gunpoint one Christmas Day and how I instinctively applied this aspect of gratitude, which resulted in a manifestation against all odds and one of the most profound gratitude lessons of my life. That story became a chapter in my entrepreneurial memoir.

Turn Your Situations Around—Now

Those challenges you listed for which you are not grateful? I want you to begin right now to turn those very situations around by expressing gratitude for the solutions *before* they appear. Bringing the desired result into the "now" moment by using the gratitude principle speeds our desired results to us.

Remember that what we focus on, we create. This is the perfect time to focus on the perfect result, not the problem. The more attention given to the problem, the greater chance it has of remaining. The more we focus on the problem, the bigger it gets.

As the great teacher Dr. Joseph Murphy said, if you give a taxi driver two different addresses, you will not get to your destination. Your thoughts and feelings should be aligned with the purpose you want to create. As long as you put your attention on what you don't want, you are taking energy away from what you do want. And energy transforms into matter and substance.

I challenge you to start feeling gratitude for the perfect happy solution to your situation as you take any constructive action outwardly. This may indeed be the most powerful agent for change in the Universe.

The Simplest Gratitude Prayer

If the only prayer you say in your life is "thank you," that would suffice.

—CHRISTIAN MYSTIC MEISTER ECKHART

~~~~~~~

6

The Solution to Any Problem—
How to Handle Setbacks

Okay, here's the plan. You will now learn to call on your innate wisdom and use scientific "prayer" to find the solution and create an adjustment to any kind of setback.

Now . . . take a deep breath. Get still and calm. Be still and know.

Know that everything is all right.

Everything is fine.

All adjustments that need to take place to resolve your situation are taking place now as you read this and as you accept the answer, the solution.

The first thing to do to solve any problem is to become still and quiet about it. Be open for guidance. But most of all, do not give the problem energy. Give all thought to the solution. There is *only* solution here. All is well.

Now go about your business and do your best to act like everything is normal. All is resolved. Everything is harmonized. If you really believe in "stepping out in faith"—get to work in your daily life just as you would usually do.

See the solution—the answered prayer—in your mind's eye, as already accomplished.

You don't have to know what the answer is, but you know there *is* an answer.

Ask yourself: How would I feel if the solution was at hand, if my prayer was already answered?

You can summon up all of the power necessary to create the perfect solution for yourself in this situation. What I am showing you is affirmative prayer, scientific prayer. It works.

Keep your mind totally focused on the solution now. As you do this, you will be guided to your perfect answer.

The answer is at hand. Accept it now.

Your **Trust** fund is enormous!

Only good can come from this!

Affirm now:

My **Trust** fund is enormous!

Only good can come from this!

I can't wait to see what good comes from this!

The perfect solution is here now. I accept it fully and completely. I expect only the best and I get it. And for this I give thanks.

Believe it. You will see it.

Problems cannot be solved at the same level of consciousness that created them.

—ALBERT EINSTEIN

My TRUST fund is enormous!

MARILYN JENETT
FEELFREETOPROSPER.COM

7

Faith and the Subconscious

Faith is to believe what you do not see and the reward of this
faith is to see what you believe.

—ST. AUGUSTINE

Our circumstances in life are the outcropping of thoughts and beliefs that have been gathered and accepted in our subconscious mind throughout our lifetime. As long as those same beliefs exist, circumstances are perpetuated and remain the same. In essence, everyone already has faith. For instance, someone who has never experienced abundance and wealth still has faith—their faith is in scarcity and lack.

Subconscious Resistance

Now, in order to experience abundance and wealth, one must shift those subconscious patterns and beliefs to faith in abundance and wealth. You know the glitch: The subconscious mind does not like change and will resist new thoughts or ideas that are opposed to what has been firmly entrenched. The subconscious mind keeps our heart beating, our lungs breathing, controls our autonomic nervous system, and retains the perfect memory of every cell in our body, but it also keeps those negative thought forms that have been fed into it deeply ingrained and static.

One cannot just decide consciously to have faith. As I mentioned previously, the conscious and subconscious minds must agree on an idea in order for that idea to come to fruition and become your reality. So if you consciously want something, but your subconscious does not believe you have it, then you will not have it.

Subconscious Acceptance Through Faith and Repetition

There are two ways in which new ideas can be accepted by the subconscious mind—through faith and repetition.

Faith

Let me give you examples of faith as it applies to our study . . .

In France, there is a legendary fountain at Lourdes, where spontaneous healings have reportedly occurred. How does this happen? The waters in the fountain are not creating the healings. When someone steps into the "holy water," their faith and expectancy produces a reaction in the subconscious mind, which has the perfect memory of every cell in their body, and a healing is produced. It is their *faith* in the healing power of the waters that really does the healing.

Another example: A parent, in a moment of anger, might say to a child, "You're stupid and you'll never amount to anything." The child may live throughout adulthood according to that belief and never know why he or she cannot succeed—all because the element of faith was involved. In this case, it was emotional impact and belief in the parent's authority that caused the child to accept the statement in faith subconsciously. Unfortunately, far too many people are experiencing lives that are the result of such childhood influences, whether subtle or severe. Many of my own private students told me of these childhood experiences.

Repetition

Subconscious beliefs can be changed through the repetition of the desired ideas. You are currently experiencing the effects of thoughts and words that you have been repeating to yourself and continuously reinforcing. These ideas keep feeding themselves and your circumstances remain the same. You are in essence "hypnotized" by these thought forms. It is vitally important that you learn how to create and instill new information in your mind to create new circumstances. That's where knowledge comes in—the knowledge to shift the faith factor in the direction of prosperity and the feeling that you are indeed the child of a Universe that is willing to provide and fulfill all your needs.

Once the subconscious shift occurs—and it can happen "in the twinkling of an eye"—your new consciousness is free to grow and expand into a greater and greater realization of the abundance that is in the world and your right to receive it. As your faith increases, so does the size of your prosperity container (consciousness).

Yes, It's There for You, Too!

Most people already know that wealth and abundance exist. They just don't accept that they exist for them personally. That's where knowledge and prosperity principles come in. But in order to expand your consciousness and change your circumstances, you must be sincerely ready and willing to change. You must have an open mind and not be stuck in a state of hopelessness and defeated by what has occurred up until now. You must have even the slightest feeling that there is something better for you, and if it can happen for someone else, it can happen for you. If someone can transition from extreme disadvantage in the ghetto to fantastic wealth and success, isn't it likely that someone with a better start could expand their mind to create more? There is a way, and it doesn't matter who you are or what your life circumstances have been. You **can** overcome past life conditions and beliefs.

Everyone already has faith. We all have faith that the sun will rise, don't we? (Well, except for the rare doomsdayer.) So, you already have faith. The important thing is: In **what** do you have faith? And what can you do to change the focus of that faith?

You simply apply the techniques that you are learning in this book to gently shift your subconscious beliefs so that they agree with your conscious wants and desires.

As within, so without . . .

8

In the Beginning Was the Word

The foundation of the Feel Free to Prosper teachings is the Word.

Whether we have a religious affiliation or none at all, at some point in time, we have probably heard . . .

> *In the beginning was the Word, and the Word was with God, and the Word was God.*
>
> —JOHN 1:1

Now, since Feel Free to Prosper is not a religious teaching, but is based on spiritual law . . . for our study, let's substitute the word "Law" for "God":

In the beginning was the Word, and the Word was with Law, and the Word was Law.

In the beginning lessons of the Feel Free to Prosper teachings, a primary purpose is to help my students come to a clear-cut understanding and grasp just how powerful their word is—the spoken word and especially the written word.

Our words become our "claim"—the imprinting of our desires on Universal Mind Substance—our claim to our natural inheritance. Our word is the bridge between our heartfelt desires and our Creator—God, Universe, Spirit, Infinite Intelligence, Divine Mind, Lord—Law—which has the ways and means, the know-how, to turn our words into "flesh."

Our word is our manifesting connection to the Lord—Law—of our being. Our word becomes flesh (form, material) when we make—and stake—our claim with faith and expectation. Our word is the manifesting mechanism in our fulfillment factory. Our word becomes the law of our being.

When we say on one hand that we want this thing but continue to express words that represent the opposite of our desire, we succeed in perpetuating the same unwanted conditions and we do not reach our fulfillment, or freedom state.

When we say on one hand that we want this thing and also say and write and express words that represent our desire, we succeed in creating space for that desire to rush in and we attract it and reach our freedom state. Our word becomes flesh—our physical, tangible, fulfilled desire. In more "clinical" terms, we have then succeeded in creating an agreement of the desired idea between our conscious and subconscious minds. And when both aspects of mind agree on the same idea, our desire becomes manifest.

We cannot have it both ways. We cannot want one thing and express its opposite and expect the powerful laws of the Universe to work on our behalf.

You cannot claim to feel "prosperous" and then state that there is no way to pay your bills. That very statement will ensure that the way to pay those obligations will not get through to you. Those words have now become your law—and beautifully represent a law of lack—your self-fulfilled prophecy.

The law never stops working for you. And you can't stop using it. But you can keep using it to manifest what you do not want, or you can learn to use it purposefully and in alignment with the abundance that universally exists for everyone, including you.

I cannot teach these principles and at the same time watch on as students express the very opposite of this powerful principle. That would be inauthentic on my part, as a devoted teacher of the laws. But more importantly, it will not help them or others who wish to become aligned with the laws. So I am quick to alert a student if I feel he or she is not aligned with the fulfilling law of their being. It is not that I am without empathy or compassion. They are very important parts of my path. But my mission is to teach you the power of the words you choose.

So the very best in empathy, compassion, or inspiration that I can offer is to firmly encourage you to choose your words and language as if your life and conditions depend on them.

Because they do.

You say that you need an answer. There is **always** an answer. There is always a solution. The Universe and the Law have ways that you could never imagine. But you must invite these answers and solutions with your words.

We are not lying. We are not ignoring reality. We are creating a **new** reality—the reality that we truly desire. Our words create our feelings. Our words and feelings create our reality—a reality that is moldable and always subject to change. What an amazing realization! We must do our part and then the Law of our being will do its part. Our words will not "return to us void."

Our word is the manifesting mechanism in our fulfillment factory.

MARILYN JENETT
FEELFREETOPROSPER.COM

9

You Don't Attract What You Want, You Attract What You Are

On a discussion forum, someone mentioned "rolling with the punches" in life. Another member responded . . .

"Marilyn will have to validate this, but as I understand the law of attraction, if you choose to 'roll with the punches,' the Universe will likely give you punches to roll with. How funny is that?"

So of course I just had to join in and quipped . . .

"I wonder what happened to all the viewers who watched over and over again that longtime TV commercial with the catch-phrase: 'How about a nice Hawaiian Punch?'" ☺

Now, the real topic of the discussion was: "Do you ever think about what you want your life to be like in one year? Five years?"

The prosperity teacher in me saw a real challenge in this question and I had to jump in. This may seem a bit profound for you if you are new to these principles, but read it over a couple of times. You'll get it.

Take a moment to think about this question: When we "want" something, what is the message that we are giving to our subconscious mind and to the Universe?

Let's consider the answer based on these statements from a previous chapter . . .

"The subconscious mind will create for us and attract to us those circumstances that it accepts to be true in the present moment."

"And what we are thinking and feeling **now** is what determines our future, its outcomes and experiences. We create that future right this moment."

Quite simply, when we "want" something, we are telling our mind that we don't have it. And the law is that we attract what we already "have" in consciousness.

Dr. Joseph Murphy:

"We don't attract what we want, we attract what we are."

It took me years to **really** get that. We attract what we are—*in consciousness*. That's it. So the way to really manifest our desire is to convince our subconscious that we already have it. Dr. Murphy said, "Feel the joy of the answered prayer." If we live in the state of the fulfilled desire, feel the reality of the goal accomplished, this will impact the subconscious.

That's the most profoundly effective key to manifesting what we want.

Living the Desire, Not Wanting It

In my mentoring groups, I conducted an exercise. Even though I am not here with you in person, you can still absorb these ideas and apply them on your own.

First, I guide my students to reach a certain state of mind. I have everyone imagine that all of their needs and wants are met in this moment of time—mentally, physically, emotionally, financially, spiritually—I want them to let go of all sense of "needing" or "wanting" anything and in the **now** moment feel complete satisfaction, complete fulfillment, complete relaxation.

So now there is nothing to want. However, in this fulfilled state, they can create anything at all. The nature of life is to continually expand, grow, and create. So if all of our desires were fulfilled, the next step would be to create something new. When we attain a goal in life, we always aspire to reach another goal. And in this relaxed, calm state we can create—without static and distraction from negative, contradictory thoughts or feelings.

When the students reach that completely fulfilled state, I have them select one thing that they desire to create in the near future. But here's the key: I have them create it in consciousness—in thought and feeling—existing **now**. Again, there is no "wanting," "needing," or "desiring." There is only the creating—in that moment. There is only experiencing the creation itself. There is only *accepting*.

I guide each student to create their scene and describe it to the others as it is happening in that moment—but it is important for them to get "out of their heads" and become completely involved in their feelings as they experience the created event. Whenever they describe details like they are "out there," I gently guide them back to what they are feeling in that moment as the event is happening around them. They are immersed in the role. They are the actor in their own play, immersed in their feelings. The results are notable—tears of joy, overwhelming feelings of happiness, and profound feelings of gratitude.

These students are **living** their desire, not wanting it. Why would we want something that we already have? I instruct the students to repeat this creative exercise as they fall asleep at night. This is the way to impregnate the subconscious mind and to bring the creation into existence in the physical world in the shortest time.

Here is one of the most interesting aspects of this manifestation process: When this does happen—when our creation does appear physically in our world—it won't even seem like a manifestation. It will seem completely natural, like there is nothing unusual going on. This is because we have already accepted our desire in consciousness. The subconscious has accepted it as a natural occurrence and it feels like the normal flow of things. But then we look back and recall the process and say, "Wow, I created that—first in consciousness, then it appeared in my world." We then fully understand the meaning of "You don't attract what you want, you attract what you are."

Words and affirmations are powerful—you have heard me say that. But just **one** moment of feeling the reality of your fulfilled desire is more powerful than a thousand affirmations.

So don't "want" it. Own it. Be it. Experience it. Accept it.

One of the greatest teachers of manifestation, Neville Goddard, advised: "Ask yourself, 'How would I feel if . . . ?'"

How Easy Is This to Do?

Please do not feel discouraged if you are not able to apply this principle right away. If it were that easy to do, then with the vast amount of knowledge and countless books and programs available today, every seeker would be walking around consistently manifesting whatever they want.

That's why I believe so strongly in a step-by-step process for overcoming the resistance in the subconscious mind and why the Feel Free to Prosper program lessons are applied at intervals to allow the subconscious to become fertile and more receptive to the advancing lessons.

In this book, I am presenting a broad foundation of the prosperity laws, followed by the specific Lesson One program at the end of the book. After applying the lesson material, you will find that many of these concepts will become easier to understand and apply.

~~~~~

10

Are You Visualizing "Out There" or from Within?

Visualize: To see or form a mental image of.

Does visualizing create a challenge for you? Many people visualize by looking at their goals "out there" on the screen of space in their imagination or on "dream" or vision boards. This chapter will explain the most powerful way to visualize and the fastest way to manifest results—visualizing from "within."

Let's discuss a bit about visualizing . . .

First, let me start by noting that some people cannot visualize in mental pictures. There is nothing wrong with this—it's just the way their brains function. But they can visualize by "feeling" the reality of the goal they wish to attain. In fact, I believe that the feeling aspect of imagining is much more powerful and magnetic than the picturing aspect.

You can feel the emotions even if you cannot see images. What is important for you to know is that *your subconscious mind cannot tell the difference between a real and an imagined act.*

Looking "At"

Now, you can make mental pictures or gather specific details and create a vision board to establish your goals in your subconscious mind. These techniques are often recommended as a way to condition the subconscious, and they have some benefit. They will encourage you to focus on what you want.

However, I have a very different opinion about visualization which, for our purposes, will include both the picturing and feeling aspects.

Let's say you close your eyes to see yourself achieving a goal. You see yourself "out there" on the screen of space, watching yourself going through the motions, almost like watching a movie.

Or you make your vision board, dream board, or treasure map—or whatever you wish to call it. You are looking at items on this board that you wish to possess, or you may have pictures of yourself on this board doing or being what you want. However, you are still looking at yourself "out there."

Again, this may have some benefit, especially if visualizing in this way produces in you a corresponding feeling of having what you want.

Looking "From"

But . . . here is the *most powerful way to visualize* and the fastest way to manifest results.

You visualize from "within." You are the actor in the role, seeing the world through your own eyes, looking out at the world as if you already are what you want to be or already possess what you desire. You assume this role and "live" in this consciousness over and over until it feels natural to you. As you rehearse this role, your subconscious will accept it and it will become your natural state of being. You will take on the mental and emotional state of the end result and then . . . at just the right moment you will experience this reality in the outer world. The outer world must conform to what you have accepted inwardly.

It's Already Mine

So here is the difference. Let's use "Bev" as an example with a relatively simple desire.

Bev wants a new digital camera.

Bev can picture the camera she wants. She can paste up photos, study it in detail, and commit the image to memory. She may even suddenly see these cameras all over the place. But will she accept subconsciously that this camera is hers? Maybe.

Or Bev can play the role. Become the actress holding the camera up to her eyes, feel herself focusing "her" camera on her subject, maybe even feel the slight weight of the camera in the carrying case as it swings against her as she walks. She can close her eyes and feel herself placing her camera in its spot on her shelf at home. If Bev were not able to make mental pictures clearly, then all she would need to do is create the feeling that she already possessed her camera—the feeling of satisfaction of owning the camera. Not desiring or wanting it . . . because if you already have something, then you wouldn't desire or want it, would you?

Bev, the real Feel Free to Prosper student who inspired this example, also put a photograph of the *back* of the exact camera she wanted on her computer desktop, where she saw it every day. This made it easy to visualize being "with" the camera, since the buttons and features became familiar, so the reality arrived very quickly.

Become the actor in the role, playing the part of being, doing, having whatever it is you want, from the inside out. From within your own consciousness, you already **are** that person, you are already **doing** what you want, you already **have** what you desire.

That is true visualization.

11

<hr/>

Your Words . . . and the Law
of Cause and Effect

I love to share those subtle gems that I have learned over the decades from my study and application of mental and spiritual laws.

Yes, some of these principles can be very subtle, but when we become aware of them, they can greatly add to our understanding of the circumstances in our lives. We must become more acutely aware of the law of cause and effect. We must become aware of the tremendous power behind our words, especially when strong feelings are attached to them. By increasing our awareness, we refine our character and our personality to become more aligned with the laws of life and are then able to attract and manifest more of what we want in life.

We cannot escape the law of cause and effect. We might get away with rolling through a stop sign and cheat the man-made laws (and that may even be in question), but we cannot do this with the laws that govern our existence.

The reason that we are not generally aware of the repercussions of this law is because of the time factor.

For example, let's say that you bump your arm on an object. A bruise may not show up on your arm until later, sometimes even days later. But this is a perfect analogy of the law. The bruise is an obvious effect from a cause that occurred earlier.

I explain to my students that the situations in our lives today are the effect of causes that occurred at some earlier time. Sometimes a cause can create a reaction in a very short span of time. Often the root cause goes back much further in time. And sometimes there can be an almost instantaneous result—we have all heard the term "instant karma."

One of the secrets, then, to manifesting what we want in life is to make sure that our **current** thoughts and feelings are in alignment with everything that is wholesome, positive, and loving—and focused on what we want to create—definitely not on what we *don't* want to create or continue creating.

The stronger our negative emotional reactions are to a situation, the more quickly and deeply they will create a new neural pathway in our brain. Once that pathway is created, it will continue to attract more of the same kind of situation. We will keep attracting more of what we don't want. Ugh!

Words are powerful. Words plus emotion are more powerful. Words that are written are even more powerful. Words written publicly that are seen and read by a multitude of people have so much power that it's like staking a public claim in Universal Mind. You certainly don't want to have that much power rebound and boomerang back to you.

What if you have to address a negative situation? I'm not saying that we should not write letters or use words to correct situations, state our case, or stand up for our rights. But it's the thought, intention, and emotion that are behind our words that we must be aware of. We can stand up for our case, we can offer feedback and criticism that is constructive, we can ask for refunds or restoration—and we can do it gracefully and with civility—without hurtful intention or personal malice. We will find that our situations will be resolved so much more quickly and peacefully and we will not make ourselves vulnerable to the law of cause and effect. And of special importance, we can become teachers and wayshowers instead of victims.

The effects in our lives do not generally have the same specific details as the causes—they may show up in different forms—but the fact is that they **will** show up in some form. We cannot escape the law.

There is one way, however, that I believe we **can** overcome the effects of our past and present "causes" or "karma"—and it is the only way that we can do so.

It is called living under the law of *grace*, and the only way that we can live under grace and not under the law of cause and effect, and settle our karmic "debts," is through . . . **Love.**

12

How Do We Eliminate Fear?

You know, when I first began my journey to find a place for myself in life and the business world and to overcome financial limitation, I didn't set out to become wealthy or make a million dollars. Oh, that was a nice dream to aspire to, but I knew that wasn't the real answer to my prosperity.

So what *was* my goal?

Quite simply . . . what I wanted more than anything in the world was to lose the fear. I wanted to feel a sense of security—the feeling that I would always have what I need and that whatever I needed would be provided. I realize now in retrospect that what I really yearned for was to be connected to my true source of supply.

Somehow deep within, beyond my limited conditioned thinking, there was a part of me that knew that the secret to unlock my freedom was to eliminate fear in all areas of life, including those financial-based fears.

So I made a decision years ago that I would no longer keep company with fear, and I have stayed the course.

Someone posted on a forum that her answer to the fear

situation was "just not letting it control you." I disagree. I believe that "just not letting it control you" is meeting fear halfway, and still allows it to keep us from our full potential. It cuts us off from our universal source and the ability to manifest what we want—an ability that is founded in faith, not fear.

We can make the decision to eliminate fear from our life. And once we commit to do that, amazing things happen and we can discover our true strengths.

I'm not saying we shouldn't feel emotions like excitement, anticipation, adrenaline rushes, and such. I'm saying that I believe that we can decide which emotions we want coursing through our mental and physical being. Do we want emotions that will nurture our spirits and bodies or ones that play havoc? I came to the realization that there was no upside to fear and I made a decision. That was the turning point.

These brilliant minds said it best . . .

I have learned over the years that when one's mind is made up, this diminishes fear; knowing what must be done does away with fear.

—ROSA PARKS

If you are distressed by anything external, the pain is not due to the thing itself, but to your estimate of it; and this you have the power to revoke at any moment.

—MARCUS AURELIUS

When the imagination and will power are in conflict, are antagonistic, it is always the imagination which wins, without any exception.

—ÉMILE COUÉ

Every Day in Every Way . . .

I speak about Émile Coué in my programs. You may not recognize his name, but you will probably recognize his gift to us. He is the renowned French psychologist and pharmacist who produced healings in patients by having them apply his autosuggestion, "Every day in every way, I am getting better and better."

Coué taught us that the imagination always wins over will-power. Our mind—our imagination—should always be focused on thoughts that represent what we want, not on what we don't want. Not only will repeated suggestion trigger the body's natural healing mechanism, it will also guide us to inspired outer action and stir up universal forces in our favor. We should always think of ourselves as happy, healthy, and successful—and confident and faith-filled, rather than fearful.

Coué also taught us that it is impossible for us to think two thoughts at the same time. Contradictory thoughts will not be accepted by the subconscious, but dwelling on a single thought will penetrate and be acted upon. Which thought will you choose?

So, What Can I Do to Eliminate Fear?

First, make the decision that you are going to do so. A firm decision—not a halfhearted one.

Next, you are going to change your words and your thoughts to instill in your deeper mind—your subconscious, your imagination—the idea of what you *do* want.

What is the opposite of fear? The opposite of fear is faith:

1. Firm belief in something for which there is no proof.
2. Complete trust and expectation.
3. Something that is believed, especially with strong conviction.

This kind of faith is based solely on our mindset, belief, and expectation—and the belief itself produces a result. Think about, bring about.

You have unwavering faith in the "absolutes" of existence—you are certain that the sun will rise or that gravity is completely reliable. But you also have had faith, or strong convictions, in circumstances, conditions, and appearances that are later proven to be wrong.

Most likely, you are living below your potential because of faith based on deep-seated beliefs that were instilled in your mind from a very young age. You may even have faith that you are filled with fear!

So we know that the mind cannot hold two thoughts at the same time and that two opposing thoughts will not be accepted by the subconscious. Therefore, the answer to this whole "fear" dilemma is to saturate your mind with words and thoughts that represent what you do want to create.

Start now by eliminating the word "fear" from your vocabulary. Begin repeating words like "confidence," "faith," "peace," and "poise." Repetition will drop these desired ideas, these seed thoughts, into the subconscious, and your mind and life will shift in the direction of these new dominant thoughts. You will acquire a new habit—a faith and confidence habit that will replace all fear.

That is the antidote for fear.

I challenge you to do it and to see what happens.

Fear knocked at the door. Faith answered. There was no one there.

—ANONYMOUS

13

The Law of Reversed Effort

Did you know there is a law called the Law of Reversed Effort? It states that the harder you "try" to do something, the less chance you have of achieving it. Trying implies a negative, it suggests to the mind that you may not accomplish. Even Yoda in *Star Wars* recognized this truth when he wisely said, "Do or do not. There is no try."

We "plant our seeds" in preparation. We want our desired result to grow and manifest just as the seed planted in the ground becomes a plant or a flower. So we first do our job and plant our seeds. We nurture the soil with positive thoughts and expectation— the water and sunshine for our mental garden. Then we turn the job over to Universal Mind—to the creative forces. We can relax and let go. Our manifestation will come.

Here is a simplistic, concrete example of how this works: Ever misplace your keys or another object? You try and try to figure out where it is, but you can't. But the moment your attention is somewhere else and you stop thinking about it and forcing the answer, the answer suddenly pops into your mind. Well, this principle can apply in a much broader scope to your everyday life and business.

Did you ever have an important problem to solve and tried everything to find a solution, but to no avail? Then, if only from sheer exhaustion, you gave up. Suddenly the answer appeared.

We might say that in order to reap, there is a time to sow— and a time to let go.

14

Forget the How and Enjoy
the Wow—Starting Now!

Forget the "How" and enjoy the "Wow" . . .

I blurted this out one day and I thought to myself, what a simple reminder the Universe just handed to me to share.

Once you have instilled in your deeper mind the idea of what you wish to attract, you must be able to let go of the *How* in order to manifest and enjoy the *Wow*.

Remind yourself that focusing on the *How* will only serve to close off the unlimited number of channels of which you are not aware. Focusing on the source of your supply will open potential channels that you could never even imagine, but that are there for you. The Universe is the source of your results, not the individual channels.

We must do our part by deciding what we want and using the mental and spiritual tools to plant the seeds of our desire in our garden. It is then time for us to let go and allow the Universe to do its job. We nourish our soil with faith and expectancy, just as a planted seed is nourished with water and sunshine.

But we do not instruct the seed on how it should grow. We don't keep digging up the seed to see how it's doing, to check to see if it has grown. We don't hover over our garden with impatience. We don't try to force our seeds to grow. With our earthly gardens, we can easily let go and trust that all of the elements necessary for the growth of our seedling will be provided by the Presence that knows just how to turn that seedling into a fully manifested flower or plant.

If you will realize that the soil of your subconscious mind is your mental garden, you will understand that you may plant your seeds and then surrender to that All Knowing Presence to bring your manifestation to fruition—in the right and perfect way and at the right time. It knows exactly what to do. It knows exactly what adjustments must be made, what elements must be harvested, and just when to bring it all together. It is the Master Planner. It is the Chief Operating Officer. It is the Project Manager.

It knows **how**. You do not. It knows **how** to open doors without one whit of effort on your part. It knows **how** to "nudge" you from within and cause you to intuitively put forth effort when required—fruitful effort that will result in your manifested desire. All of the brainpower, computer power, and genius in the world combined do not know **how** to manifest like this Infinite Intelligence does.

When you find yourself wanting to intervene in the work of the Divine Designer, please remind yourself to butt out and say to yourself:

Forget the How and enjoy the Wow!

15

~~~~~~

Loose Lips Sink Ships: Why Silence Is Golden for Manifesting

As someone who has studied, applied, and accomplished using mental and spiritual laws for decades, I have come to believe the following:

There Is Power in Silence

Manifesting power comes from your personal connection with the universal source of all good, not from others—even though they may be harmonious and supportive. It is primarily a matter of keeping the energy contained and focused, which increases the creative and manifesting power of Universal Spiritual Substance. By sharing our intentions, energy is dissipated and the focus is compromised. It is in the dark silence of the soil that the seed begins the process of creation and, having been acted upon by the creative substance of the Universe, grows into the beautiful flower for all to see.

We should not announce our pending manifestations to others. Keep silent about your results and goals until they are consummated. Manifestations can be very exciting and you may want to share as soon as they begin, but don't announce them until they are completed. This will keep the energy focused like a laser beam and maintains your clear connection with the Universe through the completion stages. This keeps our reliance where it belongs—on our Source. So wait until the completion, until contracts are signed or agreements confirmed, until it's a "done deal."

Unconscious Agenda

Maintaining silence also prevents us from being influenced by the unconscious agenda or negative opinions of others.

Others may consciously wish you success, but their deeper agenda may not be aligned with your goals and desires. This may not be intentional, mind you, but it does exist—even among family members. For example, a family member may love you and want you to be successful, but unconsciously feel that if you achieve success, they will no longer be needed. A friend's insecurities may trigger envy of your potential success. It's not unusual for others to subdue your enthusiasm, even thwart your attempts, because of their own limiting beliefs or lack of ambition. It's not necessary to understand the psychology behind these situations, but it's important to be aware that they do exist.

Secret Inner Place

A biblical scripture seems to describe this spiritual law perfectly:

> *But you, when you pray, enter into your closet, and when you have shut your door, pray to your Father which is in secret; and your Father which sees in secret shall reward you openly.*
>
> —MATTHEW 6:6

I interpret this to mean that we should go within to our *secret inner place* and take our desires to the Father (the Law, God, Universe) who sees in secret, and this Power will fulfill our desires and we will be rewarded openly when everyone sees our results. In other words, share your vision with the Creative Power of the Universe, ask for guidance, and you will attract the right people and the right circumstances to help you fulfill that vision. Let your intuition, not your intellect, guide you to those people with whom to share.

It's fine to share your progress with your personal mentor or coach. In a personal mastermind or prosperity group, sharing your personal or business goals is fine, as long as each member is supporting the others.

I find that I manifest quickly and easily using this principle, and one of the greatest lessons I have learned is to keep quiet. I created a reminder for myself—I borrowed that old World War II slogan, "Loose lips sink ships." It means, "Beware of unguarded talk." It was meant to keep one from speaking of ship movements, as this talk could be overheard by enemy agents who might intercept and destroy the ships.

The slogan has remained to this day as an admonition to avoid careless talk in general. And it does the trick for me by keeping my manifesting energy focused and in "safe" territory.

My students' experiences have further supported this aspect of law. I teach them not to share a result until it's fully consummated.

Once your manifestation is complete, then it's great fun to shout it from the rooftops!

16

How Long Does It Take for a Thought to Reach Fruition?

How long does it take for a thought to come to fruition? How does *time* relate to the outer manifestation of our thought, intention, or desire?

I have had manifestations come to fruition at the speed of light—yes, when it happens that fast, it seems like it. But I think we can agree that for the majority of results, there is a required gestation period.

My experience has shown that the time element for the physical manifestation of a thought or idea depends upon several factors:

Our Belief in What the Time Duration Will Be

The majority of people cannot grasp the possibility that something can manifest immediately, or very quickly. They have a preconceived idea of the amount of time they think it could or should take in "real-world" time. And that can potentially translate into a self-fulfilled prophecy.

Our Ability to Release the Result

Holding on to it, clutching it, analyzing it, obsessing over it, forcing it, attempting to control it by ourselves . . . these will all delay the manifestation. When we release it and let it go, we invite the Universal Creator to take over. Again, we can compare this with planting our seed in the garden of our mind, nourishing it with faith and expectation, and releasing its growth to the Creative Intelligence that knows exactly how to develop it.

The Elements to Be Aligned by Creative Intelligence

Once we conceive an idea, there are elements that we are not aware of that begin to move toward us and the fruition of our idea. There is such a thing as perfect timing for an idea, just as there is perfect timing for the growth of a seed to a plant. So the speed of fruition may also depend upon the availability of the specific elements necessary for fruition. There is often a waiting period for the elements to align perfectly. I call this "synchronicity."

Our Trust

When we trust in the entire creative process (this is related to *release*), we are relaxed and confident, which speeds up the manifestation.

Our Acceptance of the "Done Deal"

When we think and feel that our idea has already come to fruition—that is the fastest way to bring it into reality. We start with a vision for the so-called "future." In consciousness, remember, there is only **Now**. So by accepting our idea as completed, as a done deal, we are compressing time and eliminating the "bridge" from Now to that future result. In my opinion, that is absolutely the fastest way to overcome delays and bring a desire to fruition. When we succeed in doing this, we will no longer care about the time element, because in our thoughts and feelings, what we want is already happening for us. We don't desire something we already have. We are in the mental state of living it. We are relaxed and confident as we await its physical arrival.

And it rushes to us at the speed of consciousness.

17

Bless It and Praise It

What is one of the most powerful, healing, adjusting, attracting, and energizing principles in the Universe that can turn any circumstance or situation around, no matter how extreme or hopeless it may appear?

It is the principle of blessing and praising. What is so unusual about the idea of blessing and praising in these situations? Well, it is easy to bless and shower your praise upon all of the good people and experiences in life. But have you ever thought of blessing difficult people or negative situations? Did it ever occur to you to bless or praise your lack, your need, your difficult partner or spouse, bodily ills, or bank account?

Bless:

1. To invoke divine care for ("bless your heart").
2. To praise, glorify.
3. To speak well of, approve.
4. To endow, favor ("blessed with ability").

Praise:

1. To express a favorable judgment of; commend.
2. To glorify, especially by the attribution of perfections.
3. To express praise.

Well, now you are going to get into the habit of blessing and praising all of those things that need changing or healing in your life.

As an example, let me explain what happened in my corporate business over the years. I admit there were times when I wasn't content in my former events business . . . there were times when it was so busy that the amount of detail was overwhelming or I yearned to do something different or my feet hurt from overseeing a large event, even with adequate help. My spiritual side craved peace and serenity, but the big bucks came from large, precisely coordinated parties and events for corporate and convention clients.

If I stayed in a critical mood, my business came to a standstill. Now, that got my attention! So I would begin to bless my business. I would bless it and praise it for giving me the opportunity to work independently for myself, for working with talented vendors, for great clients who always paid me before the events(!). I blessed the business, the income, and the clients. I would repeat often to myself or aloud, "I bless my business and my wonderful clients"— even if there were no clients at the time. Clients always arrived.

There are many areas of life that need our blessing, and when we do give it, those areas will adjust, change, improve, grow, and heal right before our eyes. Here are some of the ways you can apply blessings and praise and watch the transformation.

DIFFICULT PEOPLE: Your spouse, partner, children, relatives, coworkers, business associates, employer, employees, creditors, debtors, landlord, tenants, strangers, and motorists.

FINANCES (OR LACK OF): Your checkbook, bank account, wallet, purse, investments, savings account, debts, invoices, and credit cards.

HEALTH AND APPEARANCE: Any body part or organ (diagnosed or undiagnosed illness), aches or pains, your physical appearance, weight, flaws and imperfections (perceived or real).

CAREER, CREATIVITY: Your job, business, or profession, creative talent, business talent, products or services, clients, customers, vendors or suppliers, teachers, and students.

LOVE LIFE: Your spouse or significant other, your singleness if you don't have a partner, your future lover or spouse (and of course bless and release the past ones!), your friends and special people in your life.

NATURE: Pets and all living creatures, plants, greenery, and flowers.

BELONGINGS: Your car (I always bless and praise my car), furnishings and appliances, computer, clothing, all belongings.

FOOD: Food that you consume and the wonderful variety of foods available on our planet, in your garden, and on your trees.

PROBLEMS: All problems and dilemmas, great or small.

It is a common spiritual practice to bless and give thanks for our food, but how many of us really do this? Blessing the incredible food available to us helps this food to be assimilated and nourish our bodies properly. This carries a spiritual vibration into the very cells of our bodies.

You can bless your problems right out of existence. Every problem contains a lesson and the opportunity for you to grow. When you use spiritual principles to solve and overcome a problem, there will no longer be a need for it to reappear in your life. Spiritual solutions produce healing—a cure, not a band-aid.

Unity minister Catherine Ponder has a wonderful way to transform negative situations with people. She recommends the use of the following affirmative blessing:

I bless you and bless you for the goodness of God (Universe, Spirit) that is within you.

I believe a similar blessing can be used for any person, situation, or object. Everything that exists—animate or inanimate—is made up of vibrating energy, and I believe that energy will respond to the "frequency" and the *frequency* of our blessing.

18

Let This Speak to Your Inner Child and Reignite the Magic

When We Were Children . . .

It's been done again and again . . . more than we adults remember
or realize . . .

> *"There is no use in trying," said Alice, "one can't believe impos-*
> *sible things."*
>
> *"I dare say you haven't had much practice," said the Queen.*
> *"When I was your age, I always did it for half an hour a day.*
> *Why, sometimes I've believed as many as six impossible things*
> *before breakfast."**

There were surprising places where the magical truth was
actually revealed to us as children in our formative years, but we
grew up in a world of mass mind negative thinking and the magic
appeared to be gone.

Maybe a journey back to what we consider "children's tales"

---

* Lewis Carroll (Charles Lutwidge Dodgson), *Through the Looking-Glass*
(McMillan, 1871).

would reveal to us a much greater wisdom at work—wisdom that our all-too-soon-to-be adult reasoning minds could not retain.

And if we come full circle, then maybe . . . just maybe, we can return to that wisdom and appreciate the profound truths that were screaming for our attention even at a delicate young age.

The Magic of Words . . .

For instance, as children, weren't many of us fascinated with magic? I remember my parents took me to see the famous magician Blackstone perform. Later, *Houdini* was one of my favorite movies.

One day I happened upon an editorial of a book for magicians titled *Magic Words: A Dictionary*, which is described as "a one-of-a-kind resource for magicians and word lovers, exploring the most intriguing magic words and phrases from around the world."*

This paragraph caught my eye . . .

> *There is profound meaning in the clichéd image of a magician pulling a rabbit out of an empty hat with the magic word "abra-cadabra." The magician is speaking an ancient Hebrew phrase that means "I will create with words." He is making something out of nothing, echoing that famous line from Genesis: "Let there be light, and there was light," only in this case the light is a white rabbit and perhaps a flash of fire. The magic word, whether it be abracadabra or another of the magician's choosing, resonates with the audience because there is an instinctive understanding that words are powerful, creative forces.*

---

* Craig Conley, *Magic Words: A Dictionary* (Weiser Books, 2008), p. 19.

In the Arabian Nights tale of *Ali Baba and the Forty Thieves*, "Open Sesame" is the magical command that opens the door to the treasure-filled robbers' den.

A magical password. But "Open Sesame" has stayed with us for ages and taken on a generic meaning. The dictionary describes it as any very successful means of achieving a result.

Yes, the truth was there for us as children, but we grew up in a world of negative thinking and the magic was gone. We forgot. We forgot how to believe. Or rather we learned how to believe in the wrong things.

But the most profound truth of all is that the magic is never gone. It is *always* there, awaiting our recognition.

We must return to the magic. We must open our minds. We must practice. We must regain respect for the power of our words.

Half an hour a day, six impossible things before breakfast, is a good start. ☺

Speaking of a Good Start . . .

I received this email from an early student of mine:

> Hi Marilyn,
> I just had to share this with you. It was on the news yesterday (maybe you saw it) . . .
> A young boy, 5 years old, wished for a dog, had been saving his money for two years and saved $200.
> When Hurricane Katrina hit, he decided to give all of his money to a charity. Well, the news about this got out and he was given a puppy (by whom I forgot) and it was a cute **white** puppy.

Here is the catch: For two years he always referred to his future puppy as . . .

"Marshmallow."

I just loved this story.

Linnea

Return to the magic . . .

19

Faith and Prosperity Consciousness

My teachings are not based on religion. They address the spiritual nature of life and the laws that encompass all people, all faiths, and all belief systems. It doesn't matter whether your beliefs are religion based or you have no religious affiliation at all. The laws are impersonal and will work for you, because they are aligned with your spiritual nature.

I believe that spiritual laws are included in all great religions, but are often misinterpreted or distorted.

For example, I have noticed how easily some people can quote phrases and scriptures from the Bible that relate to money and wealth, usually with a negative connotation. And yet they somehow seem to overlook other scriptures of equal importance that can balance the perspective in the positive. The following will present my views and address the difference between faith, spiritual faith, and religious faith. The topic then evolves into the subject of money and faith . . . and religious-based distortion.

If you are religious, this chapter will have special significance for you. I hope you find the information enlightening or, at the least, provocative enough to contemplate. My desire is that this will give you a sense of security in reaching for spiritual knowledge outside of your own religion, as well as the understanding that the universal nature of these teachings will not conflict with your religious beliefs, and will more likely create a greater understanding of them.

Faith, Spiritual Faith, and Religious Faith

FAITH

> *Faith is to believe what you do not see and the reward of this faith is to see what you believe.*
>
> —ST. AUGUSTINE

DEFINITION OF FAITH:
- Firm belief in something for which there is no proof.
- Complete trust and expectation.
- Something that is believed, especially with strong conviction.

We give of our time, talents, and services, and have faith that reward will be returned to us. We have unwavering faith in the "absolutes" of existence—we are certain that the sun will rise or that gravity is completely reliable. But we also have faith, or strong convictions, in circumstances, conditions, and appearances that are later proven to be wrong. We may also be living below our potential because of faith that is based on deep-seated beliefs that were instilled in our mind from a very young age.

This kind of faith is based solely on our mindset, belief, and expectation—and the belief itself produces the result. Think about, bring about.

SPIRITUAL FAITH

> *Now faith is the substance of things hoped for, the evidence of things not seen.*
>
> —HEBREWS 11:1

DEFINITION OF SPIRITUAL FAITH:
- Belief and trust in mental and spiritual laws.
- Belief in a Higher Power: God, the Universe, Infinite Intelligence, Divine Presence, Spiritual Substance.

We base our expectations on the mental and spiritual laws of the Universe, such as the law of cause and effect (karmic law), the universal law of circulation, the law of giving and receiving, the law of reciprocity, the law of increase. As you sow, you reap.

We can take this a step further and base our faith on our perception of a Higher Power—God, the Universe, Infinite Intelligence, Divine Presence, or Spiritual Substance—as the source of our constant and never-ending supply. We place our complete reliance and trust in the source of all good, and know that we are connected to that source as the child of a rich Universe.

> *For it is the Father's good pleasure to give you the kingdom.*
>
> —LUKE 12:32

RELIGIOUS FAITH

> *I come that ye may have life, and that more abundantly.*
>
> —JOHN 10:10

DEFINITION OF RELIGIOUS FAITH:

- Belief in the traditional doctrines of a religion.
- Strong belief and conviction in a system of religious beliefs.

Now, the definition of faith that we embrace in our prosperity work and in our study of universal laws is that of spiritual faith. The elements are not based on organized religion. However, the elements of spiritual faith may be and often are included in a particular religion or its doctrines.

For example, Feel Free to Prosper teachings might be described to a Christian with the following scripture:

> *And do not be conformed to this world, but be transformed by the renewing of your mind.*
>
> —ROMANS 12:2

The scripture clearly lets us know that we have something to do with the creation process—and that "something" relates to our thoughts and feelings.

The Feel Free to Prosper teachings are about renewing our minds and overcoming faulty beliefs in the subconscious that keep us from being aligned with our spiritual source. That source—however you perceive it—is the source of everything we desire and awaits our recognition.

I often use the term "Universe" to allow a majority of people to relate. Everyone on this planet has a right to understand the prosperity laws and to receive the gifts of their spiritual heritage. There are many different paths to the One Source that has many names.

Religious Faith and Prosperity Consciousness

It is important for the growth of our prosperity consciousness for us to be discerning and become aware of religious dogma that may have conditioned our minds, even unconsciously, to interfere with our acceptance of true prosperity in life.

A businessman student of mine was raised as a Catholic and wrote to me about the words of the liturgy in the Roman Catholic Mass, just before Communion.

"Lord, I am not worthy . . ." begins the verse. He stated that he probably uttered this several hundred times decades ago. Considering that the subconscious mind does not reason but accepts our words literally, how do you suppose such a repeated utterance affects one's ability to prosper in life?

"Money is the root of all evil."

This is one of the most misquoted verses in the Bible. The actual verse is . . . *For the love of money is the root of all evil.* This means we are not to "worship" money as our God and that we are to remember and acknowledge the true source of our wealth. And indeed, we must "love" money if we want to attract it into our lives. We recognize it as another form of spiritual substance that emanates from our universal source of supply.

"Filthy lucre . . ."

The Latin root of *lucre* or *lucrum* also means "avarice" and meant "shameful or illicit gain." Now, think about it. Money can be no more "filthy" or "evil" than the sheep or other livestock or grains or metals used as a value of exchange for trade in ancient times before "money" appeared.

You can see how centuries of misinterpretation can tar the

meaning of words and phrases, which can result in a profound impact on the prosperity consciousness of millions of people.

Acknowledge instead the spiritual literature, such as the following biblical references that offer the proper perspective and assure you of your birthright to prosper:

For it is he who giveth thee power to get wealth.

—DEUTERONOMY 8:18

For then thou shalt make thy ways prosperous, and then thou shalt have good success.

—JOSHUA 1:8

All things whatsoever you pray and ask for, believe that you have received them, and you shall have them.

—MARK 11:24

I hope this has given you something to ponder carefully with regard to your personal faith.

Part Two

Feel Free to Prosper—Your Finances

The amount of substance (wealth) that we have depends upon how big the container (consciousness) is that we bring to the ocean of abundance. We can bring a spoon, a cup, a pail, a tank. The challenge is to acquire the tools to enlarge our container.

—MARILYN

Since I began teaching prosperity laws, I discovered that not only the general population, but even those who have a strong background in metaphysics, prosperity teachings, the law of attraction, etc., have deep-seated barriers to attracting money.

In Part Two, you will come to understand the underlying cause: a belief that there is a separation from the source of our supply—our "invisible means of support." You will see that true security is not related to our bank accounts and financial assets.

I want to inspire you to recognize that the negative thoughts about money do not reflect a person's true nature. They do not represent the talents, the abilities, the qualities, or the essence of the person you truly are. On the contrary, they represent negative false beliefs that were acquired throughout a lifetime and that were instilled in your mind at an early age by others. We recognize the false beliefs about money and prosperity for what they really are— the lie! The truth is then revealed that through our connection with the unlimited source of supply, each and every one of us can prosper.

In this section I teach that the "real you" has access to all of the creative forces of the Universe, because each person is an individualized expression of Universal Mind, Infinite Intelligence, God.

You will learn exactly how your conditioned thinking, habitual words, and even criticism of money perpetuate your financial lack. You will learn how to quickly shift your focus to create new patterns of thought and speech to begin to magnetize money instead of repelling it.

By practicing the principles presented, you will be applying the prosperity laws directly to your finances to acquire a true sense of security and establish your connection to your continuous source of supply.

The success of my teachings is largely based on the ability to get my students to subconsciously accept financial prosperity as an existing reality—the ultimate key to manifestation. The techniques and their application will fulfill the promise.

You will also be excited to learn how one of the great perks of acquiring a prosperity consciousness is that savings and discounts and bargains of all kinds will follow *you* on the path. Suddenly it seems like the Universe becomes your personal shopper whose goal is to provide you with the best for your needs at the very best price.

If you are a parent, you will understand how your use of words can mold your child's future and what you must know and do to ensure that your children grow up to become happy, prosperous adults.

A special highlight of this section: You will learn the single most **immediate** thing you can do—right now—to increase your income . . . and it has nothing to do with the outside world!

20

~⌒~

How Much Money Do You
Really Need—or Want?

As a teacher of prosperity principles, I have met and mentored people from all walks of life, or we might say, "all walks of consciousness."

I have had students with $5 to their name and in dire circumstances, who learned how to have their needs met and find joy in that accomplishment. I have had students who went from modest means to millionaire status and, although grateful for that accomplishment, desired to attract even greater riches. Of course, the great majority of my students are somewhere in between.

I have given a lot of thought to this money thing—or, more accurately, this desire for money thing.

When I started out on my quest for a prosperity consciousness and a better life, I didn't plan for millions. My primary desire was to lose the fear—the fear of not having enough, of not having my needs met, of being like my parents, and of living a life of lack and not moving forward. My real quest was for a sense of security—not the false security that comes from having money (and yes, I finally came to believe that it is indeed a false sense)—but the security of being connected to the greater Source of all good, the Source of perpetual supply. I yearned to be so connected that I would be in a peaceful and constant state of trust. In the words of the great Dr. Joseph Murphy, my earliest teacher, I wanted to be "fearless and free, an inlet and an outlet to the Mind of God."

A few of the quotes that I came across greatly influenced my reasoning about money:

> *Success is not to be measured by how much material wealth is possessed, but whether you are able to create at will what you need.*
>
> —PARAMAHANSA YOGANANDA

> *I've never been poor, only broke. Being poor is a frame of mind. Being broke is only a temporary situation.*
>
> —MIKE TODD, FILM PRODUCER

And one of my personal favorites:

> *The trouble with most people is that they have no invisible means of support.*
>
> —DR. JOSEPH MURPHY

All around us in society—and now predominantly online—is this preoccupation with riches. We are barraged with emails, advertisements, marketing, and sales material promising riches, success, six-figure incomes, seven-figure incomes, and on and on. It's all about getting rich. There are ongoing book releases addressing this theme—to their credit, many are also promoting values and a balanced life, but the central theme is often about getting rich and making millions.

To name just a few . . . In an earlier generation, there was *The*

Lazy Man's Way to Riches. I imagine author Joe Karbo got much richer selling his book. From an even earlier era, but rediscovered in our generation, was *The Science of Getting Rich.* The author, Wallace Wattles, lived for years in poverty but persisted in his studies of truth principles to find success in his later years. He believed that man must be rich to fully express himself in life. There is of course Napoleon Hill's classic *Think and Grow Rich,* and so many others—certainly no shortage of books and literature on the keys to riches.

When I first created Feel Free to Prosper, I met a writer in Canada. I was sharing my new lessons and principles with him. He was a good writer, lived simply amid the beauty of British Columbia, and had a very close friend who was wealthy. But he was concerned. He was middle-aged and worried about the fact that he had no desire to be wealthy like his friend. I recall that he said he was also influenced early by his father's desire for him to be "successful." He wondered if there was something wrong with him. He said he was quite happy as long as he could pay his bills, spend his time writing, walk out his back door to visit the woods and its creatures, and be able to visit his daughter and grandchildren. He wanted nothing more. I told Dave that in my opinion he was successful.

Dave's perspective only served to convince me that "success" or "riches" have as many different definitions as there are people.

Certainly someone living in a developing nation would have an entirely different idea of success than an American corporate CEO or entrepreneur. And the value of money often changes with environment and culture. I was surprised to discover that the income of an educated engineer or doctor in India might be equivalent to $2,000 for a month's salary. So much for the value of the American dollar!

I recall stating to students of mine that if I were speaking to them on the telephone from a million-dollar yacht rather than from my living room, I didn't believe I would be one whit happier than I was at that moment. Oh, I might be inclined to throw yacht parties on occasion, but I don't think it would make me "happier."

I have thought a lot about this idea. How much happier would I be with greater and greater riches? Surely I agree that with money, one can be exposed to and enjoy much of the world and its beauty. I think we should love money and should have money. After all, it's our right to be prosperous. This work to which I am devoting my life is an offshoot of my own desire to claim my good from the universal supply. But just how much money—riches—do I need? How much do I want?

How much money do *you* need? How much do you want?

Does the idea of riches beckon because of the proliferation of marketing promises? Does it seduce you because you feel that if someone else can have it, then why can't you? Have you been influenced by family or friends to stretch your limits? Or influenced by others in the opposite direction? Does "riches" symbolize security or happiness to you? Does it symbolize power? Freedom? The ability to provide for your heirs?

Does money promise to fill an empty emotional or spiritual void? (It won't.) Or do you even require riches at all? Does a simple, uncomplicated life have more appeal?

Please consider your most intuitive, heartfelt answer—not the one based on society's expectations or a false sense of worthiness based on the size of your financial assets.

In the current economy, I have seen people interviewed who have lost their lavish lifestyles to more humbling situations, only to discover personal and family values that had been previously missing. I have also heard stories in the past of successful men and women who, in a good economy, quit their high-paying careers with all the trappings to open a flower shop or bed-and-breakfast and discover their joy in a simpler life.

I have asked myself: How many homes do I need? How much clothing? How much can I travel? How many investments are enough? Would I want more riches because that's what everyone says we are supposed to want? How much money do *I* really need or want?

Please don't misunderstand. I am certainly open to all the wealth the Universe showers upon me. But the way I see it, wealth serves two primary purposes:

- Freedom.
- The ability to help others.

That's my bottom line.

How about you? Can you be completely honest with yourself about this? How much money do you really need—or want?

〜〜

21

We Need to Eliminate That "S" Word

Let's discuss the "S" word—one of those insidious words that becomes lodged in the subconscious and that keeps us from expressing who and what we really are . . .

From the time I created Feel Free to Prosper, a lot of my written material has been triggered by comments on the social networking forums that I visited. I am grateful for this because my desire to help others has allowed my most valuable insights to surface.

One day a woman expressed that she felt that her struggles are making her a better person. If you have a similar belief about your life circumstances, please pay close attention.

I do not believe that your struggles are empowering you to be a better person. I believe somewhere along the line that specific belief was instilled in your mind and it may have become an excuse for *not* overcoming the "struggle" mentality. Yes, it's a mentality. Whenever I speak with someone, I recognize their subconscious mindset within minutes into our conversation—and why they are not moving forward in the way they want. This is revealed by the words that spring up repeatedly in the conversation—words that they are usually not aware of saying.

One of the most common culprits is the word "struggle." I

don't see any real need for that word. I think it should be eliminated from our vocabulary—especially if we intend to grow a
prosperity consciousness.

We were not brought into this life to struggle. Really. Well,
maybe making our entrance from the womb wasn't a piece of cake,
but we were not given a stage pass into this life so that we can
struggle to be a better person.

We Are Here to Discover Who
and What We Really Are

Do you know what the purpose of your struggle is? The purpose
is for you to become aware of the laws that govern your existence
so that you will break through that consciousness and shine your
light. It's a wake-up call. It is a sign that you are not aligned with
your true purpose and your natural inheritance from the source of
all good—and that it's time to change your situation and learn to
receive what is rightfully yours.

It is our soul revealing to us the *mirror* of our consciousness
so that we will take the action to create a new *reflection*. It is our
spirit telling us to come up higher, that there is more to life than
that "S" word.

I will share something personal. I used to kick and scream and
rail against struggle. Or rationalize it. I went through so much to
learn how to accept and receive. But one of the enlightening moments in my life was when I realized that human beings feel they
have to suffer and feel pain before they can receive their answers.
We don't understand that it is our right to receive by what we call
grace.

I am so grateful for the moments when I finally got it. I "got" that I didn't have to kick and scream or do anything at all to make something happen or become better. I could just relax and trust and my answers would come, often at the speed of light. Wow . . . I didn't have to pay for it by struggling. What a concept!

Although struggle *can* be a part of growth and enlightenment, we will only continue to experience it until we realize that it is no longer necessary. We can come above those "growing pains," so to speak.

Struggle may deepen our compassion and empathy—I have no doubt about that because it worked that way for me. However, we do not need to hang on to it. Once we learn to connect with our Source and receive our good, we can release struggle entirely and use our understanding to help others if we so choose.

By the way, I am not just referring specifically to struggle in financial situations. This can apply to all areas of life.

If you love scriptures, here is one that beautifully addresses the topic, and the words of a great American poet who had her own unique "spin" on this concept:

Consider the lilies of the field, how they grow; they toil not, neither do they spin: And yet I say unto you, That even Solomon in all his glory was not arrayed like one of these.

—MATTHEW 6:25–34

"Consider the lilies" is the only commandment I ever obeyed.

—EMILY DICKINSON, AMERICAN POET

22

Loving Money

Let's start out with the negative ideas we don't want to say and hear, but that may hit home and cause you to take stock . . .

- Do you criticize money in thought and speech?

- Do you speak negatively of your bank balance or business income?

- Have you thought of money as a "necessary evil," "the root of all evil," "filthy lucre"?

- How do you feel when others have more money than you do?

Well, now is a good time to take stock of these patterns and understand once and for all that any of these ideas will certainly prevent the flow of prosperity to you.

Dr. Joseph Murphy taught that if we criticize money, it will fly from us.

Why Is This So?

Remember that what we focus on, we attract. If you focus on not having enough money, you will continue to not have enough money. If you envy someone else's money, you are really telling your subconscious that you don't have any. Your mind accepts the same message if you live in a state of fear about money or give money a negative connotation. Remember, spiritual substance responds to our words and thoughts. Money has no more negative attribute than gold, silver, wheat, sheep, or any other form of value exchange ever used.

Are you a gardener? Do you believe that when you love your plants, you nurture them and they are happier and healthier plants?

How about your children? What happens when you love them and nurture them? Is there anything you can think of in your life that does not grow and prosper when showered with love and blessing and praise? If you love your body, it will respond with health and vitality. If you love your work or your business, it will grow and prosper. Well, you can also love money right into your life.

We must heed Dr. Murphy's words. We must learn to love money and stop criticizing it. That means to love your checkbook, your bank accounts, your online statements—everything associated with money. Love money and you will attract it. Anything that you love, praise, and bless will grow and prosper—be it human, animate, or inanimate. Spiritual substance responds to our blessings and love.

Think of the larger vision. Aren't you learning to literally *embrace* your prosperity?

Lighten Up!

It's important to lighten up and have fun with money, too. The more fun you have with prosperity, the faster it will rush to you.

One student feared looking in her checkbook. I asked her to think of her checkbook as having human characteristics and feelings—as a feeling, animated object that didn't want to be rejected and feared. It wanted love and appreciation. We laughed, picturing her checkbook wanting hugs. She released her fear of looking in her checkbook. She was well on her way to attracting money so that there would be even more in her checkbook to love.

Another student visualized checks jumping and running "with glee" into his pockets. This was an Internet businessman who used his quirky sense of humor consistently with the Feel Free to Prosper lessons to attract money. He even entertained us by singing his affirmations to the tunes of famous nursery rhymes like "Pop Goes the Weasel" and "Frère Jacques." It worked! His sales kept increasing.

In the recorded Feel Free to Prosper program, I have a set of Prosperity Boot Camp Drills that everyone recites together, military-style. The drills are effective because the subconscious mind responds to rhyme and rhythm. We "sound off" together in perfectly uncoordinated fashion, but the fun and laughter it creates is priceless. Learning to lighten up and have fun with prosperity to replace a somber attitude will speed your results.

Do these methods feel silly? Will you feel silly loving money? Maybe. Why not? I say, feel silly all the way to the bank.

Love money and have fun with it—and have fun earning it, attracting it, even winning it. The more fun you can have with prosperity, the more you will attract.

Yes, you can love money—pure spiritual substance in the form of money. We have discussed what happens if you don't love money. If you criticize money, you will repel it. If you buy into some antiquated belief that it is the root of evil or filthy, you will repel it. If you envy someone else's money, you will repel it. If you are afraid to go to your checkbook or bank account to see the balance, you will repel it. If you are in a constant state of worry or fear about money, you will repel it.

Isn't it time that you became a **magnet** for money and prosperity? Isn't it time for you to learn to **love** money? How about starting now?

~~~

23

What Actually *Is* Money?

Here is my definition of money, through the words of Charles Fillmore, cofounder of the Unity spiritual movement. These excerpts from his works are also included in the Feel Free to Prosper Lesson One material that you will be applying:

> The spiritual substance from which comes all visible wealth is never depleted. It is right with you all the time and responds to your faith in it and your demands on it. It is not affected by our ignorant talk of hard times, though WE are affected because our thoughts and words govern our demonstration. The unfailing resource is always ready to give. It has no choice in the matter; it must give, for that is its nature. Pour your living words of faith into the omnipresent substance, and you will be prospered though all the banks in the world close their doors. Turn the great energy of your thinking toward "plenty" ideas, and you will have plenty regardless of what men about you are saying or doing.
>
> There is no scarcity of the air you breathe. There is plenty of air, all you will ever need, but if you close your lungs and refuse to breathe, you will not get it and may suffocate for lack of air. When you recognize the presence of abundance of air

and open your lungs to breathe it deeply, you get a larger inspiration. This is exactly what you should do with your mind in regard to substance. There is an all-sufficiency of all things, just as there is an all-sufficiency of air. The only lack is our own lack of appropriation.

The spiritual substance is steadfast and immovable, enduring. It does not fluctuate with market reports. It does not decrease in "hard times" nor increase in "good times." It cannot be hoarded away to cause a deficiency in supply and a higher price. It cannot be exhausted in doles to meet the needs of privation. It is ever the same, constant, abundant, freely circulating and available.

All manifest substance flows from the realm of light waves, according to the findings of modern physical science. One or more light particles, electrons, form the atom that is the basis of all physical manifestation.

Man must build a perfect soul structure with faculties capable of always producing abundantly for both his spiritual and his material welfare. In order to accomplish this man must become familiar with what the metaphysician terms omnipresent Spirit substance, which is visible only to mind and the nature of which is to sustain and enrich whatever idea is projected into it.

This Spirit substance stands back of and gives support to man's every thought and word. It is ready to provide food for all living creatures everywhere.

Today man is learning consciously to make union with this invisible spiritual thought stuff and appropriate and manifest it. Our supply and support is governed by our familiarity with substance and by our mental hold upon it. Spiritual substance is the source of all material wealth and cannot suffer loss or destruction by human thought. It is always with us, ready to be used

and to make potent and fertile both the soul and the body consciousness.

Just as the earth is the universal matrix in which all vegetation develops so this invisible Spirit substance is the universal
matrix in which ideas of prosperity germinate and grow and
bring forth according to our faith and trust.

If we are to go forward spiritually, we must not waste our
thought stuff in idle thoughts, in thinking thoughts of poverty,
discontent, jealousy. We should positively weed out of consciousness all thoughts of poverty and failure, and in thinking or
speaking of our affairs we should use the very highest and best
language at our command.

Whatever the seed word is that is implanted in omnipresent
Spirit substance, this seed word will germinate and grow and
bring forth fruit "after its kind." Just as the farmer therefore
selects the very best seed corn for planting, so we must choose
the words that will bring forth the rich harvest of plenty.

To gain control of Spirit substance we grasp it with our mind;
that is, lay hold of the idea back of it. Right thinking is necessary
in using the mind constructively to bring about right results.*

Now, doesn't this description of spiritual substance suggest
a Divine form of love—the love of the Creator for its creations
"ready to provide . . . for all living creatures everywhere"? I can
think of no higher form of love than the Love that Spirit holds for
us. And all we need to do is open our minds and hearts to the
Divine gifts. And included in those gifts is money.

---

* Charles Fillmore, excerpts from *Prosperity* and *Teach Us to Pray*. Used with permission
of Unity, www.unity.org.

24

Reality Check—Whose Reality Is It Anyway?

In the beginning of the Feel Free to Prosper program, I ask my students to explore and share their core feelings and beliefs about their relationship to money and prosperity.

Now, this is a *real* reality check—or we might call this a prosperity reality check.

If you think that in some way life has stacked the odds against you, if you feel that there isn't a level playing field for success, if you feel challenged in your ability to succeed, then I strongly recommend that you not only read my words carefully in this chapter, but also review the biography at the end of the chapter—the biography of a woman who, in my opinion, is one of the greatest inspirations of all time.

Whose Reality Is It Anyway?

So, let's say that you have discovered your core belief (or beliefs) about money and prosperity. Now what are we going to do about it?

Well, first I am going to tell you the important truth about those negative beliefs. The truth is . . . *your beliefs are a lie*. A lie.

The interesting part is that as long as you keep accepting those beliefs, they remain *your* lie that colors and predicts your reality, so in essence they become *your* truth. That is, what you believe to be true. Your life experience is the outcropping of your accepted (false) truth. Your circumstances and outer "appearances" only serve to perpetuate this "truth" and to further "prove" that it is so. And thus the lie keeps feeding itself. You are hypnotized.

Then, when you attempt to consider the possibility of abundance and success for yourself, that's when you feel like you are lying to yourself.

Well, I have news for you. Those beliefs that you have expressed are not at all related to the real you. They are not who you are. They do not represent the talents, the abilities, the qualities, or the essence of the person that you are—the real you.

They represent negative false beliefs that you acquired throughout your lifetime and that were instilled in your mind by others, even when you were very young. You unconsciously made those beliefs your own.

The nature of the subconscious mind is that it will create and produce for you according to the ideas it has accepted as reality.

The real you has access to all of the creative forces of the Universe because you are an individualized expression of Universal Mind, Infinite Intelligence, God. That intelligence gave you your talents and abilities and also gave you the means to fulfill those talents and abilities.

So I Ask You . . . Whose Reality Is It Anyway?

How do you tune in and become who you really are?

The first step to victory is to recognize those false beliefs for what they are—the lie. They are *not* the truth about you. They are the lie. The fact that you cannot attract money or clients or success in your business is a great big lie.

I would like to go back in time here . . .

One of my early students was owed quite a bit of money from a former employer and they had refused to pay for over a year. Any effort she made to collect failed. Then we met and she began the Feel Free to Prosper program. Shortly after the second lesson, she was able to get a mediation date in court. I prepared her for this welcome opportunity. At the court proceeding, the insurance company for the employer adamantly refused to pay, although my student carefully kept her cool and focused her attention on prosperity thoughts as the attorneys and judge interacted. The judge finally said he would take the ruling under submission until the following week, but it was obvious that the employer's representatives were not budging.

My student had to wait for an entire week and insecurities started to set in. Her core belief was that she was meant to struggle, that "winning" this ruling in her favor would be too good to be true. She said she kept hearing an inner voice telling her this.

Although I normally endorse using only positive words in our study and don't even like to use the word "lie," I found myself spontaneously telling her that what she was hearing was that old subconscious "tape" playing over and over in her mind and that she must recognize it for what it was—**it was the lie!** The truth was that she is a child of the Universe and entitled to all of the supply and abundance that she could have if she could keep her mind open to receive.

That did it for her. Whenever those old conditioned thoughts would come, she would remind herself that *that* was the lie and she would again become centered.

Here is the story in her own words as posted on the Feel Free to Prosper forum:

> Hello fellow financial coaching groupies!
>
> I had a productive week in regards to our lesson plans and tangible results. Shall I say more???!
>
> When I saw Marilyn's announcement of the FFTP program, I just knew that it was the perfect pole vault to take me over the top. It was just a gut feeling. I am moving into a new phase of my career and Marilyn's insight and solid lesson plans were just the right distraction to bring me to the next level. And thus far it's succeeding. Without getting into too much mundane detail, I had a leftover challenge from an employer of more than one year ago. They owed me $$, refused to pay, and I was determined not to give back my income to them by walking away because there was a clear right and wrong issue here.
>
> Well, after a year, I finally got my "day in court" so to speak (more of a mediation). What was exceptional is that I had just gotten Marilyn's second lesson and had gone over half of it when this happened. The day in court was long and arduous. Also exceptional was what I did with my time. I relied heavily on my affirmations, and during long periods of time when I was alone and the pressure was on, I developed a meditation that was inspired by Marilyn and our Lesson Two. I focused on an object and really felt, thought and visualized that I was a magnet for lots of money and that the magnetic energy that I was putting out there was getting stronger and stronger. When I got nervous, I would move back into that space of just concentrating on the magnetic energy

I was giving out. When negative thoughts would trickle in, I would just tell myself that they are a "lie" because they are! That was customized by Marilyn for me and was of enormous help. Several days later, I found out that everything was settled and I got a big chunk o'money!! Now with that chapter behind me, I can clearly focus on my career goals in terms of financial success. I can't wait for the next lessons to unfold!

Thank you, Marilyn!

Now, here are some more **truths** about your negative beliefs— one or more of these may apply to you:

- You are comfortable with them. After all, they are familiar, aren't they—even if you weren't aware of what they specifically were, they have become "second nature," haven't they?

- You might feel you are stuck with these beliefs—there is nothing you can do about them so you might as well make the best of it.

- These beliefs might provide the excuse or justification for not moving forward, even not succeeding.

- You might feel that if you just keep going along like you are with these beliefs, things will just get better somehow and you might have some lucky breaks to get you where you want to go.

None of these factors will produce money and success for you. You must now make a conscious choice to become aware of your false beliefs and recognize them for what they are—blatant false beliefs. Lies that you no longer wish to apply to your life and that in no way serve you.

You must take the upper hand and make a stand for what you want to create in your life. It is a choice. It must no longer be an unconscious choice. It must be a conscious choice and you must now become the boss. You and only you must decide . . .

Whose Reality Is It Anyway?

If the following biography does not touch and inspire you in some way, then I will admit that you are beyond the scope of my abilities as a mentor. But I am certain you will understand why I am including this . . .

Helen Keller (1880–1968), is an outstanding example of a person who conquered physical disabilities. A serious illness, which her doctor called "acute congestion of the stomach and brain," destroyed her sight and hearing at the age of about 1½. Because of this, she could not speak and was entirely shut off from the world. But she rose above her disabilities to gain international fame and to help disabled people live fuller lives.

For almost five years, she grew up, as she later said, "wild and unruly, giggling and chuckling to express pleasure; kicking, scratching, uttering the choked screams of the deaf-mute to indicate the opposite." Then Helen's father took her to Alexander Graham Bell. He advised Keller to write to the Perkins Institution for the Blind in Boston (now Perkins School for the Blind in Watertown, Massachusetts). Shortly before the child was 7, Anne Sullivan arrived from Boston to teach her. Sullivan had been nearly blind during childhood, but surgery in 1881 and 1887 partially restored her sight. She later married John A. Macy, but she remained with Helen Keller until her death. Then Mary Agnes "Polly" Thomson, who had been Keller's secretary, took Sullivan's place.

She Learns to Write. Sullivan was able to make contact with the girl's mind through the sense of touch. She used a manual alphabet by which she spelled out words on Helen's hand. Gradually, the child was able to connect words with objects. Once she understood, her progress was rapid. Within three years, she knew the alphabet and could read and write in Braille.

She Learns to Speak. Until she was 10 years old, Keller could talk only with sign language. She decided she would learn to speak and took lessons from a teacher of the deaf. By the time she was 16, she could communicate well enough to go to preparatory school and to college. She chose Radcliffe, from which she graduated in 1904 with honors. Sullivan stayed with her through these years, interpreting lectures and class discussions for her.

She Helps Others. After college, Keller became concerned with the conditions of the blind and the deaf-blind. She became active on the staffs of the American Foundation for the Blind and of the American Foundation for Overseas Blind. She appeared before legislatures, gave lectures, and wrote many books and articles. She started the Helen Keller Endowment Fund and asked for funds from wealthy people.

Keller became especially interested in bettering conditions for the blind in developing and war-ravaged nations. An enthusiastic and untiring traveler, she lectured in their behalf in over 25 nations throughout the world. During World War II (1939–1945), Keller worked with soldiers who had been blinded in the war. Wherever she appeared, she brought new courage to blind people.

Keller received many awards of great distinction. They included the Chevalier's ribbon of the French Legion of Honor, the Alumni Achievement Award of Radcliffe College, and decorations from many governments.

Keller's books have been translated into more than 50 languages. They include *The Story of My Life* (1902); *Optimism* (1903); *The World I Live In* (1908); *The Song of the Stone Wall* (1910); *Out of the Dark* (1913); *My Religion* (1929); and *Midstream: My Later Life* (1930). *Teacher* (1955) tells of Sullivan. The motion picture *Helen Keller in Her Story* told the story of Keller's life. The play *The Miracle Worker* (1959) and its motion-picture adaptation (1962) described how Sullivan made contact with Keller through the sense of touch. Helen Adams Keller was born on June 27, 1880, in Tuscumbia, Alabama. She died on June 1, 1968.*

Again I Ask . . . **Whose Reality Is It Anyway?**

---

* "Keller, Helen" from *The World Book Encyclopedia* © 2007. By permission of the publisher. www.worldbook.com. All rights reserved. This selection may not be reproduced in whole or in part in any form or format without the prior written permission from the publisher.

25

Why My Law of Satisfaction Works Faster Than the Law of Attraction

I created a new universal law. Well, actually I think the Universe created it and just decided that I would be the one to teach it. And here's how it goes . . .

I believe that when most people address the law of attraction, they do so with the belief that they don't have what they want—that they want to attract it. If we desire something, if we want something, if we want to attract something, what is the message that we are giving to our subconscious mind?

There is only one reason you do not have what you want.

You do not have what you want because your consciousness is filled with the *thought* of not having what you want. As long as the thought of *not having* remains in your mind, you will continue to *not have*. So if you accept this premise, then the way to have what you want is to change your consciousness to the thought of *having* what you want.

The reason you have not had the prosperity you desire is because there is faulty subconscious conditioning related to this. Somewhere along the way you have accepted as fact the idea that you are not prosperous. Everything that happens seems to support that fact and prove that you are right, doesn't it? Well, the fact is that everything that happens in your outer world is mirroring to you exactly what you have accepted in your inner world—your subconscious mind. Your circumstances are reflecting back your deepest beliefs at that moment.

Now, this is the harsh reality: As long as you continue to believe the same fact in the present moment, conditions will remain exactly the same and you will continue to have the same experiences. You know that expression, "Same old, same old." You are on automatic pilot. You feel helpless.

Help Is on the Way!

The techniques you are learning and applying are helping to create a subconscious *acceptance* of your prosperity. When you have accepted the fact that you are prosperous, money will come to you as naturally as the sunrise. Struggle will cease to exist and avenues for prosperity will open to you effortlessly.

Note that I said *are* prosperous, not *will be* prosperous. That's right. I said when you have accepted the fact that you *are* prosperous. **Now.** This moment. Until you feel that you are prosperous and have money now, in this very moment, you cannot be prosperous. Let me repeat that. Until you feel that you are prosperous and have money *now*, in this very moment, you cannot be prosperous. That's the law. I didn't create it. That's just the way it is.

Tomorrow Never Comes

The subconscious mind will create for us and attract to us those circumstances that it accepts to be true in the present moment. Our job is to condition our subconscious mind to accept what we want as an *existing* reality. I want you to think about the following statement very carefully: Tomorrow never comes. It is always the present moment or *now* in consciousness. When what we call later or tomorrow arrives, it will actually still be the present moment. It is always *now*. And what we are thinking and feeling *now* is what determines our future, its circumstances and experiences.

Isn't it amazing, how children do not have to struggle to bring their consciousness into the "now"? They're not hung up on the past or future, on yesterday or tomorrow. They are right there now, talking to what we perceive as their imaginary playmates, totally absorbed in the present moment. A child will look at a bug and it is a monumental experience. To them that bug is the Universe.

Close your eyes (you may even be able to do this with your eyes open) and experience your prosperity like that bug. There is no yesterday or tomorrow. No *not* having—only having. You see and feel only prosperity. If only for a moment you can put aside any doubts or fears and feel the reality of this fact, create the feeling that you are prosperous, then you will have succeeded in impacting Universal Mind, the substance from which all things are created.

One moment filled with the reality of your answered prayer is more powerful than a thousand affirmations.

One great teacher said to ask yourself, "How would I feel right now if my dream were realized?" My own great teacher Dr. Joseph Murphy said, "Feel the joy of the answered prayer." Did you ever think about something you wanted and suddenly you would burst out smiling? That's the joy of the answered prayer.

I call it the Law of Satisfaction. Create the feeling of satisfaction of already having what you want and it will speed its way to you. The purpose of my teachings is to help you reach that feeling.

I dedicate this law to the words of St. Augustine:

Faith is to believe what you do not see and the reward of that faith is to see what you believe.

Repeat after me:
I deserve the best in life and I get it!

26

Prosperity Consciousness or
Bargain Consciousness?

A very good question was posted on my forum.

I thought this was an excellent subject to pursue, as I have no doubt that this subject is probably on the minds of many who desire to maintain a prosperity consciousness when outer appearances support the opposite, especially in a down economy.

Question

I consider myself a good shopper. I use coupons, wait for sales, buy generic brands, etc. But are these smart shopper "actions" sending a bad signal to my subconscious? After all, the message I want to send is "I can afford anything (at any price)." How about it, do we have to be as careful with our actions as we are with our words?

Answer

What a wonderful opportunity to express my views relating to prosperity consciousness vs. bargain consciousness . . .

On the subject of sales and bargains, there is something magical that happens when you acquire a prosperity mindset.

Have I ever mentioned to you that one of the great perks of acquiring a prosperity consciousness is that savings and discounts of all kinds will follow **you** on the path? When we are connected to our Universal Source, suddenly it seems like the Universe becomes your personal shopper whose goal is to provide you with the best for your needs at the very best price. You no longer have to shop to seek the best prices—no comparison shopping, no bargain hunting. Discounts and savings seek you and appear before you spontaneously as if you are the elite member of a private wholesale club. Except that the savings you attract are often far below wholesale!

This is not to be confused with a kind of "bargain" mentality that is based on lack and the fear of not having enough. The spontaneous manifesting of savings—the real bargains—come when we accept prosperity as natural to us and we know that the Universe is providing for all our needs. It's a joyful experience. We attract bargains at the highest possible level. We are intuitively led to the right place at the right time.

Let me share just a few of my numerous experiences of being spontaneously guided in this way to "universal"-sized bargains . . .

I have always loved beautiful, fine-quality handbags. One year I walked into Nordstrom's department store and found an absolutely gorgeous black leather and leopard-print handbag. It was extremely expensive looking, but I didn't recognize the designer name. The attached sales tag showed the price of $135—not at all unreasonable for such a beautiful bag. It was the only one of its kind in the department. I had to have it. I handed it to the saleswoman, but she looked at the tag and told me she couldn't sell it to me. She said this designer's bags sold for at least $500 or $600 and this one must have been mislabeled. Although the label was attached, she believed she was justified in refusing to sell it. The department manager wouldn't be in until the following day. We arranged for the saleswoman to put the handbag on hold and have the manager call me to give me the correct price.

The next day, the department manager called and told me the price of the handbag was $600. But since the attached tag read $135, she told me that by store policy, she had to sell the bag for the labeled price. She invited me to come and purchase my bag for $135.

I have found that expensive handbags stay new looking for years, and that one still looks beautiful to this day.

Another year I found an elegant Donna Karan Couture clutch handbag in a department store. It was $900—way beyond the price I chose to spend. But I had a "hunch" to ask the saleswoman if the bag might go on sale in the near future. For some unknown reason, she looked over the bag very carefully and found an imperceptible tiny flaw hidden in a fold that no one would ever see. I certainly would not have found it. But she said that since it had that tiny flaw, she had the authority to sell it to me at half price! I never asked for this. She offered. Another beautiful bag I still use that receives many compliments.

One of my most striking experiences was the purchase of an entire collection of Villeroy & Boch dinnerware. I didn't set out to buy a collection—I intended to buy a few place settings of the gorgeous Plantation and Tropical Collection, which was on sale in a department store's catalogue. But when I called to place the phone order, the store had none in stock. I discovered that particular pattern had been discontinued by the manufacturer and any remaining items in circulation were selling at up to 80 percent off retail prices. I jumped on the opportunity and, using only the telephone, I was guided to manifest the entire collection from several stores around the nation. The retail cost of the collection: over $7,000. The price I paid for everything: under $1,500. This included not only ten settings of the dinnerware, but all of the accent pieces, accessories, flatware, and bakeware.

Another time I was shopping for a specific item of sleepwear and didn't intend to buy anything else. But I was irresistibly drawn to a sale rack where I found two beautiful Ralph Lauren casual pieces—top and bottom—in my favorite shade of red. They were the only two items of that kind, both in my size, and they fit perfectly. They were marked down half price but I loved the outfit so much I would have paid full price. When the items were rung up at the register, the saleswoman informed me that the half-price tag was incorrect. Instead, they scanned at $6.52 each!

A major coup was when the Universe literally handed me my beautiful new car and opened the door for me to purchase it—brand-new—for about $10,000 less than retail.

Do I look for bargains? No. Do I love a bargain? Yes!

As a prosperity thinker, expect these surprises to show up in every area of your life and business—for everyday needs as well as for luxury items.

The Universe is your personal shopper.

27

Prosperity Consciousness and Our Children

During your child's formative years—up until about age five or six—they are most influenced by the words you use. And your understanding and use of words in the following years will also be responsible for molding your child's future.

Do you want to learn how the power of your words can affect your children? Are you ready to learn what you must do so that your children will grow up to be happy, emotionally healthy, successful adults? Do you want them to have a prosperity consciousness when they become adults?

And . . . just imagine how much fun it would be for your kids to be able to attract money **now**.

What is consciousness? The dictionary defines it as "the thoughts and feelings, collectively, of an individual." And philosophically, "the mind or the mental faculties as characterized by thought, feelings, and volition."

It took me decades to overcome the impact that my own parents' consciousness and belief system had on my life. I studied about the mind for years and years and applied the mental and spiritual principles to overcome the lack consciousness that I acquired from my well-meaning parents.

The study of mental and spiritual laws and prosperity consciousness should not begin when we are floundering as adults. It should begin early in our lives. Parents should understand how the mind works and the impact of their words before they decide to conceive. They should take responsibility for the beliefs they are instilling in their child's mind.

Awareness is everything. The greatest legacy you can leave your children is the gift of a prosperity consciousness. A prosperity consciousness is not just about money, although a child's beliefs about money will influence him or her throughout life. It's also about self-worth and self-esteem.

You know that deep down you want your children to have successful lives without hardship. Here is what you must know and do to ensure that your children grow up to become happy, prosperous adults . . .

- Learn how your mind works and why your words, thoughts, and emotions affect your child even before you give birth.

- Understand that the power of your words greatly impacts your children and sets the foundation for their entire future, no matter what their age.

- Realize that there are two ways in which your words impact your children on a subconscious level—through faith (strong emotion) and repetition.

- Practice the words to say to grow your child's prosperity consciousness while ensuring that he or she doesn't become spoiled.

- Teach your children the powerful principle of gratitude, which will build their character, teach them value, and also help them manifest their heart's desires.

- Know that your child can develop the mindset to attract prosperity—and, yes, money—even at a delicate young age.

- Make sure **you** develop an empowering mindset that connects you to the Universal Source of all prosperity so that you will have the ability to provide more for your family.

- And do not doubt this for a moment: Your children **will** acquire your prosperity consciousness—or lack of it.

There was a discussion about handling children and teaching them values without spoiling them. Someone mentioned that they tell their child that they aren't going to buy something for them because they don't have the money. I think that's a fairly common excuse that children are given when the parent says no.

That is the reason so many children grow up to become adults with a "lack" or poverty consciousness. It is in the formative years that those core beliefs are formed and they will often become ingrained for life. The subconscious mind does not reason—it accepts those beliefs without judgment. In the Feel Free to Prosper program, we discuss core beliefs which usually begin in childhood. I hear it over and over again from my students who have been playing out those core beliefs throughout their lives: "There is never enough money," "I don't have the money," "It's a struggle," "I can't have what I want." The list goes on—those old tapes playing repeatedly in their minds, continuing to affirm the beliefs that were instilled when they were young.

So, I implore you . . .

Learn the right words to use. Speak to your children in a way that doesn't create a lack mentality. Change **your** consciousness. Your children **will** pick up your consciousness. And the greatest gift you can give them is a prosperity consciousness.

Have the boldness to tell your child that you are not going to buy the item for them. The reason is that you are the parent (the boss) and it's because you say so. Or tell them that this is not the right time . . . maybe they can have it later. Be creative with your words. But please don't tell them it's because you don't have the money, that you can't afford it. Contribute to your child's future success and financial health by not using words that represent lack.

It was a long journey for me to overcome my own family's consciousness. Since becoming a teacher of these principles, I have seen so many people suffering needlessly because of their parents' ignorance of the way the mind works and of the power of words.

You do not have to spoil children. You can teach them values. And you can do it while planting the seeds of a prosperity consciousness in their receptive young minds.

Guess what? By watching your words and changing your delivery, you will be conditioning your own mind to prosperity— and you'll find that you **will** then have the money to purchase that item. Ah, but you can still tell them that the answer is **no**.

28

The Fruit Doesn't Fall
Far from the Tree, Unless . . .

In one of my group sessions, I shared my story of how a simple phrase my mother said to me when I was a child had an effect for half a century. She told me that persimmons made your mouth pucker. It was only when I began teaching prosperity laws that I remembered this and suddenly noticed persimmons in the markets, discovering one of my favorite, most delectable treats.

The heart-shaped variety of persimmons that should be eaten soft are only distasteful and extremely bitter if they are not ripe, but when fully ripened they are fantastic. But my mother's words stayed in my subconscious all of those years and actually "blinded" me from even noticing the fruit in the markets when they were beautifully displayed in season.

How much more powerful do you think those expressions are that we heard our parents and others say with regard to money and lack? How much time must elapse until we become aware enough to notice the opportunities and prosperity around us? Or even know they are there for us? The time is now—to raise our awareness and learn to notice, despite what we may have believed in the past.

A few days after that group session I received an unexpected package from UPS and put it aside until I returned home later that night. It was rather heavy and I just couldn't imagine what it was.

Upon opening it later, I found a crate from a Northern California company that contained the largest, most beautiful persimmons I had ever seen! A crop of persimmons was soon enticingly displayed on my kitchen counter waiting to ripen and soften. No, my mouth did not pucker, but it sure was watering in anticipation.

The anonymous note on the shipping form read: "As you manifested . . . The Universe."

One of my students had graced me with one of the sweetest, most precious gifts I could ever receive. New deliveries arrived over the next several persimmon seasons.

The recording of that group session, which had been conducted on the telephone, became part of the audio program sold on the website. I had forgotten that my persimmon story was included in that particular program until I began to sporadically receive deliveries of large crates at my front door. The Universe continued to bless me with an abundant harvest of my favorite treat!

I think my mother must be smiling in the next dimension.

29

〜〜

The Single Most Immediate Thing You Can Do—*Right Now*—to Increase Your Income

Now, based on what you have learned so far, here is a question for you:

What do you think is the single most **immediate** thing you can do—right now—to increase your income and start attracting money?

Stop reading right now and think about the answer. Do not return to this page until you believe you have it.

And the answer is . . .

The single most **immediate** thing that you can do right now to increase the flow of money to you is to . . .

Change Your Words!

Change the words that you speak to reflect those spoken by a successful person . . . a person who *has* money . . . words that represent what you want in life. Eliminate any words or phrases from your vocabulary that represent the opposite of what you want.

If you really want to increase your cash flow quickly, think and speak as if you already have that cash flow. Remember, the subconscious mind only functions in the *now*, and what you think, say, and feel right now, in this moment, is what you will begin to attract. The dominant thought in our subconscious is what determines our circumstances. So we must shift our consciousness to a new dominant thought. The repetition of positive words will eventually replace negative patterns in the subconscious, which block your success and limit your income and your supply.

If you don't want it, don't say it!

Your words have tremendous power. Believe it. Do not doubt this for a moment.

You can begin this right now, this very moment. By changing your words, you will be well on your way to changing undesirable thought patterns and changing your life and finances.

Open Sesame!

Something to Think About . . .

Every word we speak, every thought we think, and every emotion we feel is recorded in the subconscious. Through repetition or with enough faith or emotional impact, the subconscious will accept our words as a command and will create, attract, and magnetize circumstances, conditions, and persons to ensure the manifestation of our command.

Even words spoken casually can bypass the conscious mind and drop into the subconscious and take root. "The subconscious mind cannot take a joke." Seemingly harmless expressions can produce undesirable results in our lives.

How many times today have you said aloud or to yourself, even casually, "I can't afford . . . "?

Part Three

Feel Free to Prosper—
Your Business or Career

The Universe will find a way to bring us the rewards that we claim for ourselves. But we must claim it—boldly—and know we deserve it.

—MARILYN

A great deal of attention has been devoted to this section on business and career for a very good reason. A large majority of my students, clients, readers, followers, and subscribers are seeking wisdom and knowledge for financial increase, advancement, and solutions relating to their livelihoods.

There are new and seasoned entrepreneurs, "solo-preneurs," business owners, working moms, and those who have left or are leaving the traditional business arena to start home-based businesses. There are job seekers who are seeking better-paying and more fulfilling positions, professionals, sales agents who want to attract clients, as well as artists, writers, entertainers, designers, coaches, and healers. People from every walk of life are looking for answers and intuitively know that the answers are not found solely in traditional business methods. My students represent every category mentioned, and they achieve success with the same principles you are learning and the lesson material you will soon apply. You will no longer have to pursue success. You will just accept and receive it—and it will pursue you.

My teachings are based on what I call practical metaphysics: the study and application of transcendent universal principles from methods that appeal to "real-world" sensibilities—techniques that can be understood and utilized with ease. In other words, a simple approach that assures a practical application of these profound laws. I take the mystery and speculation out of these principles and instead concentrate on putting them to use—a nuts-and-bolts approach.

A fascinating component of my teachings addresses the issue about whether you can attract or magnetize circumstances without taking physical action. I discuss "right mental activity" that inspires a corresponding "right physical action/activity." But I am also adamant in stating that the process also includes sitting back and waiting for what you want to magically appear, for mental action is thousands of times more potent than physical action. That's when it really gets to be fun!

I have over twenty years of experience with these kinds of results (it's all detailed in my entrepreneurial memoir), my students have manifested in the same way, and now you, my reader, will become privy to these "nuts-and-bolts" teachings that will attract success to your business or career, often in startling ways.

This section overflows with fascinating, thought-provoking— and strikingly effective—principles and techniques that I personally utilized as the creator of a small business, a pioneer in my industry who attracted the world's largest corporations for two decades without advertising, marketing, cold-calling, or networking.

You will learn the difference between working to live and living to work, how to finally overcome fear, put a greater value on your skills and increase your income and profit, magnetize ideal clients, and thrive in **any** economy—because your dominant thought will be "progression, not recession."

And perhaps most exciting of all—you will realize that the Universe **is** the greatest marketing department, publicist, or employment agent you could ever imagine!

30

～✦～

Metaphysical Marketing

This is the first of several chapters relating specifically to the marketing of your business. Let's call this "metaphysical marketing."

The foundation of success is in your mind.

You do not need to struggle, seek, and strive to build your business or career. You can use mental and spiritual laws to create and attract all the elements that ensure success. Wouldn't you love to set your business on "automatic pilot" and enjoy the ride?

The Law of Reversed Effort

The application of prosperity principles in business allows us to become aligned with these spiritual laws to learn how to "receive" success instead of "trying" to make it happen.

Remember the law of reversed effort? It's worth repeating here. It states that the harder you "try" to do something, the less chance you have of achieving it. Trying implies a negative—it suggests to the mind that you may not accomplish. Even Yoda in *Star Wars* recognized this truth when he wisely said, "Do or do not. There is no try."

Practical Metaphysics

My teachings are based on what I call "practical metaphysics."

First, what do we mean by "metaphysical"? Well, "meta" as used as a prefix in metaphysical means "comprehensive" or "transcending." Metaphysical is relating to the transcendent or to a reality beyond what is perceptible to the senses. In other words, it's a study of what is outside objective experience. This includes aspects of the mind and spirit.

My definition of practical metaphysics is the study and application of these transcendent principles from methods that appeal to our "real-world" senses, techniques that we can understand and utilize with ease. In other words, a simple approach that assures our practical application of these profound laws. We take the mystery and speculation out of these principles and instead concentrate on putting them to use—a nuts-and-bolts approach.

I believe that there are a great number of people who have read, studied, and are well informed about spiritual matters and metaphysical laws, but who have not been able to take these ideas from their intellect and incorporate them mentally and emotionally to put them into practice.

The Universe Is My Marketing Department

Now, this study in no way discounts the marketing techniques and tools taught by the visible world's marketing experts. What I am doing here is helping you lay the foundation for a mindset that will allow you to use those tools if you so choose, and succeed with them.

Just as a house cannot stand without a proper foundation, all of the marketing, sales, and business know-how in the world will not result in success unless you first have the internal foundation—the mindset—to succeed. Once you create that foundation, you will automatically be guided to all the appropriate elements that will result in your success. You will be guided to do exactly what needs to be done to get your results. You'll find as I did that Universal Mind is truly the greatest marketing department you could ever hope for, and the possibilities are unlimited.

You can experience the guidance of an *unseen* hand, know what it feels like to live a *charmed* life, and realize that you have an *invisible* means of support.

I proved the validity of this approach to success from the fruits of my metaphysical labors in my special event business over a twenty-year span.

Now, here is a secret that you may find hard to believe. When I reveal this fact, people say, "Of course you don't mean this literally." Ah, but yes, I do mean this literally: During those twenty years, I never actively sought clients. The clients always found me. The majority of my clients were the world's largest corporations. I never advertised, marketed, cold-called, or networked. And yet my tiny one-woman company attracted these large corporate clients. Doors opened spontaneously for the right exposure, the right opportunities, and the right clients. You have to admit that something uncommon must have been involved—and that something was an uncommon state of consciousness.

This also applied to my new life and evolution as a prosperity teacher. When I began teaching the Feel Free to Prosper program, I had no idea how I would attract students or create a reputation. Once again, I took this to my universal marketing department, applied the prosperity "homework," and trusted that the doors would open. I also listened and waited for guidance. The doors opened. I had no previous experience interacting on the Internet and had never heard of social networking or social media when a complete stranger invited me to join an online networking site called Ryze.com in late 2003. I had learned to use a computer only a short time before. I participated in discussions and shared my wisdom on several networks and created my own Feel Free to Prosper Network, which soon became the platform and launching pad for the prosperity program that would attract attention from around the globe.

In 2006, I felt inspired to write my entrepreneurial memoir on my network—the story was intended for my members. But it soon attracted an agent, tens of thousands of readers, and ultimately resulted in publishing offers and the book you are reading.

I had no intention of writing a book. All of the elements flowed together as if I were under the jurisdiction of a divine destiny. I am convinced that each of us has a particular destiny to fulfill but we need to become aligned with the greater Intelligence that can guide us there.

Nothing Personal

It doesn't matter if you are a business owner, executive, entrepreneur, professional, working mom, job seeker, network marketer, sales agent, coach, or creative talent, or even in transition looking for your true place in life. It doesn't matter what your age, background, experience, or station in life is. The laws are impersonal and will work for everyone.

Here is why you should learn and apply Feel Free to Prosper principles:

- To overcome the resistance in your subconscious mind and raise your awareness to a level of consciousness that empowers and connects you to the Universal Source from which *all* prosperity flows.

- To apply this awareness specifically to the marketing and success of your business or career as you become an open channel through which clients and financial prosperity will flow easily to you.

- To come to the absolute realization that you are not alone and that you have all the creative power of the Universe ready to inspire you and guide you to success if you will only recognize and acknowledge it.

- To become attuned to your universal marketing department that will inspire you and prompt you to do exactly what you need to do.

- To prosper you in all areas of your life, not only financially, but also in health, love, relationships, and creatively and spiritually.

Okay, Let's Have Some Nuts and Bolts

1. Watch Your Speech

The successes listed above can be accomplished only through the use of positive and life-affirming language. Do not doubt that for a minute. The words you think, speak, and hear are recorded in your subconscious mind and will produce circumstances that correspond to your thoughts and speech. If you want a successful business or career, you **must** resist the habit and temptation of speaking about the lack of business or clients or jobs. I tell my students, "If you don't want it, don't say it." Even if you feel like you are lying to yourself or others, continue to speak in positive terms about your business and affairs. As you persist in speaking successful words, your subconscious will accept the new ideas and you will discover that the "lies" are becoming a new and very tangible reality. But it always first begins in mind. Never forget this.

2. Start Listening

As you develop positive thought and speech patterns, you will begin to clear the debris and static in your subconscious that has prevented you from tuning in and listening to your intuitive promptings. Practice paying attention now to those promptings, the hunches, the feelings, the "still small voice" that subtly urges you to do something. As you practice listening and following through on these hunches and the more you discover that they lead to successful results, the more consistent and the stronger they will become. You will have truly discovered your **invisible means of support**.

3. Attitude of Gratitude

You have heard that over and over again, haven't you? But do you live it? Well, start now. Remember the powerful premise we discussed that most people do not know about—expressing gratitude for what you don't yet see?

Start giving thanks **now** for your new clients, your increased business and income, your new job, and inspired new ideas—**before** they arrive. I promise if you will maintain your state of gratitude, they will come, and often at a speed that will astound you. Give thanks now for the universal guidance that led you to these words that contain truly life-changing elements.

4. Your Business or Job Is *Not* Your Source of Income

I'll bet you'll read that again. But that's right. Your business is not your source of income. Your clients are not your source of income. Your job is not your source of income. Even your savings and investments are not your source of income.

There is only one source of income. That source is *The* Source—that Universal Intelligence that you may refer to as Universe, God, Infinite Intelligence, Divine Mind, Spirit, All That Is, the Field of All Possibilities. All of those other avenues are "channels" of income, but they are not the source.

As soon as you learn to align yourself with, rely on, and trust the Source for your income, clients, jobs, and every other good thing you could possibly desire, then all of the channels will open for you to receive your good. How many channels? Limitless channels through which your supply can come to you! It is not your job to know them. It is your job to trust your Source, and as you do, both expected and unexpected channels will open and clients and jobs and ideas will increasingly come to you "out of the blue." So release all ideas that your income and business must be derived from only one particular channel.

31

Action? Or Magic?

You may have already guessed that I have an uncommon perspective with regard to marketing in business. I love the opportunities to share what I believe to be *the* most important and effective way to market a new or existing business. I am presenting wisdom gleaned from my personal experience in overcoming adversity to become an established entrepreneur. If you are not familiar with my background, in order to offer credibility for my use of the prosperity laws in business, I'd like to share a portion of my bio that was used for a women's media summit. I was invited to be a guest speaker, but I was the only "nonexpert" to speak at the summit, as I had no experience in PR, marketing, publicity, or advertising . . .

The Universe Is My Publicist

"With no publicist, PR, or marketing resources, and using only her prosperity principles and the 'Universe as her publicist,' Marilyn manifested a cover feature story in the *Los Angeles Times* that attracted thousands of telephone calls for years and syndication around the world via the Associated Press. This was followed by local and national prime time television segments and continuing media exposure, including the first article she ever wrote that grossed $250,000 for her business!"*

I like to say that my "fifteen minutes of fame" turned into a career of two decades serving the world's largest corporations. This may seem "big" to you or out of reach, but the truth is that I was just an average woman—yearning to make something of myself, but just getting by and desperately wanting to overcome a lack consciousness that had held me back my entire life. I was able to achieve victory by studying and applying the universal laws and prosperity principles that you are learning here.

This means I became aware of the importance of learning the laws of mind in order to create the mindset to attract success and market in business. There is no question in my mind that the use of prosperity principles—based on mental and spiritual laws—is by far the most valuable and effective way to market your new or established business and to achieve ongoing success.

In my entrepreneurial memoir, *Feel Free to Prosper: An Entrepreneurial Memoir of Synchronicity and Guidance,* I reveal how I applied these laws to overcome adversity and accomplish in my special events business for two decades. And then, twenty years later, I reinvented myself, found my life purpose, and created an entirely new career—Feel Free to Prosper—with these same laws.

As you can tell, sharing the importance of these principles is my passion.

A student of mine replied to a post of mine on the Feel Free to Prosper forum and inspired a dialogue. I think you'll find the conversation interesting . . .

---

* Women's Media Summit, www.womensmediasummit.com/speakers (October 2008).

Student: I **love** this post. Why? Because you add the part that I see so many prosperity teachers leave out: the action built upon the foundation of a prosperity consciousness. You say, "Once you create that foundation you will automatically be guided to all the appropriate elements that will result in your success. You will be guided to do exactly what needs to be done to get your results." I **so** agree! Sometimes people mistakenly believe that if they get right with their mind and consciousness they don't have to do anything—they can sit back and while they wait, what they want will "magically" appear. It's important to remember to build the foundation and then take action with what your intuition guides you to do. Isn't that what you're saying?

Marilyn: Yes, that's what I'm saying . . . except for this very important point: **It *also* includes sitting back and waiting for what you want to magically appear.** ☺

And that's when it really gets to be fun!

I can honestly say that my greatest successes occurred when I sat back and took no action—physical action, that is. My memoir is filled with many examples. Campbell (the soup company), one of the last clients of my special event business and one of the largest clients of my entire career, arrived when I did absolutely *nothing*. I thought I had phased out of my former business entirely. But this billion-dollar client came from a fluke phone call, not from a business source. You might argue that this was a residual effect from a previous cause—my foundation in business that was established years before. Well, yes, that would be true—but the fact is that when Campbell appeared out of the blue, I had done nothing to seek clients and I had no previous experience with the types of promotions they contracted me for. Further, I had never secured locations out of the country or booked events that required overnight accommodations. For the following three years, I secured the most exotic locations—Hollywood mansions, a castle in England, and a Caribbean island for Campbell's multimillion-dollar promotions for children. When Campbell Canada saw what I had accomplished for the U.S. market, they called and asked me to repeat these same promotions for the Canadian market! These bookings provided a wonderful cushion while I was establishing and growing Feel Free to Prosper.

There is a subtlety here that you need to understand. I also want you to trust that your intuition may at times guide you to *sit back and wait*. Actually, becoming a magnet for prosperity is action, too.

Remember that doing the prosperity work **is** taking action in and of itself. And the mental activity is thousands of times more powerful than any physical activity. But at the same time, we also remain open to those intuitive promptings that guide us to physical action. That's what we call *inspired* action.

So our results can manifest either way. We must remain open to both aspects of these manifestation laws—and realize that it's not "magic" we are referring to, but it certainly is magical. You are right though . . . the main essence of this subject is the guidance system that operates once we tune in.

Here's to everyone experiencing some magic!

Student: Well, I love the idea of a little (or a lot!) of magic! And I definitely agree that mental and spiritual homework—especially like the homework in your lessons—IS action. I have a full notebook to prove it! Thanks for the inspiration!

~~~~

32

Mental vs. Physical Activity in Marketing

Let's further explore that fascinating issue about whether one can attract or magnetize circumstances without taking "action." My intention is to create a better understanding in your mind about the use of mental and spiritual laws for success and the relationship between mental and physical action in your work.

Let's Get Mental

Yes, indeed, marketing your business is an activity. But that does not mean that the activity is necessarily "physical."

Mental activity is thousands of times more potent than physical activity. In fact, mental activity is the precursor to the right physical activity that gets results. However, physical activity is not necessarily required if you understand and apply the right kind of mental activity. It is not magic. It is law. I have always said that what we think of as "supernatural" is really quite natural once you understand the laws.

You'll realize that the Universe is indeed magnetic, and that thought and feeling have more vibratory pull than any magnet you could imagine.

So I think it behooves anyone who wants to be successful to become aware of the relationship of mental and physical activity and know when either is indicated. There is the right mental activity, which can itself attract results *without the need for physical activity* **and** there is also the right mental activity that inspires the corresponding physical action that produces results. If the right mental activity is not included, then one will end up like the majority of the population—doing and doing, acting and acting, but not succeeding.

Now, by presenting this principle to you, I am not suggesting that you spend all of your time sitting around and doing nothing. I won't address that further because I believe you'll understand the distinction of what I'm teaching you.

However, that being said, the absolute truth is . . . yes, we can attract circumstances to us without taking physical action. When you understand fully that thoughts are things and all physical things are in motion and vibrating at the molecular level, you will understand that it is indeed a magnetic Universe and we can vibrate to our good and it can vibrate to us. I know that without knowledge in this area, it may appear fantastic, but by explaining this in the simplest terms possible, I hope to create understanding and acceptance in your mind.

How Do I Know?

As mentioned earlier, throughout my twenty years as a business owner, I never looked for a client—and my clients were substantial corporations. I never advertised or actively promoted. And yet I became renowned in my field and received all the exposure and publicity I could possibly want—not as a result of anything I did physically, but as a result of the mental activity I learned to do. The physical action came *after* I attracted the clients and the opportunities. It was then that I worked to fulfill the creative vision of the clients' projects and I attracted all of the ideas and elements necessary to do the perfect job. But it was easy. It flowed. I finally learned that I didn't have to struggle or push or try or waste energy to get the job done. For the most part, the right answers truly came "out of the blue" when I was open to receive.

But the actual marketing of my business—it was always receptive, never active, except when prompted from within to walk through the doors that opened as a result of the mental activity.

I attracted national, even global publicity, with no resources or contacts in that area. I don't think I knew what a press release was! Yet, I manifested major publicity that continued for years with no work on my part. Physical work, that is. The work was done on a mental level.

Right Action

So when you apply these laws, whether from a purely mental standpoint or a spiritual basis, you are guided to the actions that are necessary because the law must produce what you have mentally accepted. You are no longer spinning your wheels—you are now on an automatic path to your results and to your success.

You use the prosperity teachings to establish—impregnate— the thought and feeling of what you want in your deeper mind. You are then intuitively guided to do all of the things necessary for the result. You follow the leads. You do the outer work that you are guided to do. You also *attract* all of the things necessary for the result. The result may indeed come without outer physical action on your part or it may require action, but the right action will be shown to you. You're in the flow.

There is a sense of connection to a source of wisdom that knows all the answers and you can tap into that source anytime you want. You will know when to be still and do the mental work and wait, and when to take outer action that results in your success.

The alternative? You work and work and struggle and struggle and don't get anywhere. And wonder why you don't succeed.

So . . . to pooh-pooh the idea of attracting and magnetizing your good—even from "out of the blue"—whether in your personal life or your business, just reveals a lack of awareness and a mind that is not open to the infinite possibilities that surround us. It indicates a mentality that is not up with the times or open and receptive to the great discoveries of our time that can further our success.

My point: You can close your mind and limit your ability to succeed. Or you can open your mind, expand your vision to include both the physical/active world and the mental/magnetic world and . . . be really successful!

❧

33

Antidote to Fear of Failure

I believe that the antidote for the fear of failure is to come to the realization once and for all that you are **not** alone in this game called life.

You have at your disposal all of the creative power of the Universe, and all you need to do is acknowledge this and open yourself to receive guidance and direction from this universal intelligence. Call this guidance, call it intuition, or call it inspiration. Call it whatever you want, but come to the clear-cut decision that it exists and it exists for **you**.

Think of the vast ocean of the Universe. You are not the whole ocean but you are a drop in the ocean—and all of the characteristics, abilities, potential, and creative power of the ocean are in you. You cannot be separated from the ocean. You are always connected to your source.

But somewhere along your path you came to believe that there is a separation, that you are not connected to your source of good. This is an illusion that was created from the negative beliefs you acquired along the way, most likely instilled in your mind by others, even from a very young age.

This was not your fault. This does not mean that you are

undeserving, that you are doing something wrong (at least consciously), or that you are not a good person—or that you are destined for failure. You just acquired false beliefs and took on the
beliefs of others who were unaware and made them your own.

It's time to recognize those beliefs for what they are and to
shift the focus of your thoughts and emotions to that intelligence
that can turn everything around—and often so quickly that it's
stunning. My own experiences of guidance and synchronicity
dramatically changed my life and all I did was what I am suggesting that you now do.

Let's say you are spiritually oriented. Well, you must have the
willingness to practice what you believe and incorporate your
beliefs into your real-world activity. When you do so, you will get
a response—and another . . . and another. That's what I call spiritual intelligence. And that is the foundation of success.

There seem to be many paths, but the quickest, most complete, and most permanent path to self-esteem, self-love, and
success is recognition of the Divinity within you. You are a spark
of the Divine. Know it.

34

Working to Live—or Living to Work?

Some time ago, a businessman and I were discussing the concept of passive income and he quoted a famous guru who stated that if you make a lot of money but have to show up to work, then you're still a slave.

I said that I didn't necessarily agree with that. I'm all for creating passive income, don't get me wrong. But when you are showing up to do the work that you love, you are certainly not a slave! Which brings to mind the subject of "working to live—or living to work," which I believe is worth exploring . . .

I believe that each of us is given special talents and gifts and that it is up to us to discover those gifts and become aligned with our true purpose. When we find that purpose—our true "work"— we are in bliss and in love with it because we are doing what we were meant to do. It could be in business, in the arts or sciences, or even being a parent.

So, in essence, we are then living to work—to express **our** work, our purpose, our joy, our bliss. That is what I mean by living to work. And I believe there is a very good chance that when we are aligned with that work, we become a magnet to the material riches that the Universe has for us, and we are open to the abundance that surrounds us.

I could never live a life doing nothing but traveling, vacationing, lunching, shopping at posh department stores, or spending hours at a country club. I, for one, will always need to be expressing myself in some joy-filled work—my soul demands it. Just like my body needs to breathe.

A very clear picture comes to mind. There is a wonderful movie, *Always*—a Steven Spielberg film and remake of the original *A Guy Named Joe*. The original is about a woman whose fiancé—a military pilot—"returns" after death to guide her to new love. In the modern version, the pilots are firefighters whose planes spray the forests to extinguish fires.

I saw a documentary about Spielberg filming the movie and in one segment he was lifted high in the sky in a crane to check out the scene and lay of the land. All around him were the blazing fires and I recall hoping they weren't real trees but props and special effects. What struck me so intensely was when he took his eyes away from his camera, stood up, threw up his arms, and yelled, "MY GOD, I LOVE THIS BUSINESS!"

That, dear reader, is living to work. Mr. Spielberg doesn't have to do this for money. He has all the passive income in the world.

Now, this subject surfaced because this businessman and I were discussing the potential for books and information products to create passive income. Those are wonderful avenues for prosperity, but for me, they don't take the place of showing up to communicate with my students or the public or exchanging prosperity energy on interviews.

This reminds me of another old adage out there—that "showing up is half the battle."

Passive income? Showing up? I say, why not have both? There are no limits in this abundant Universe.

Right Employment

If you are employed in a job and "working to live" in a position that is not aligned with your talents, your values, or your passion, it is time to consider a change. Even if it's an entry-level position, being immersed in work that you love will put the Universe on speed dial, move you up quickly, and bring fulfillment to your life. Dr. David Viscott, renowned psychiatrist, best-selling author, and media personality, once advised a radio caller in this matter. The woman was unhappy at her job—her passion was to be an artist. Viscott told her to find a job where she would be surrounded by what she loved, such as working in an art gallery. I thought this was excellent advice and in alignment with the laws—what we put our attention on, we attract.

What If I Don't Know My Purpose?

If you don't know what your right work is and are searching for direction, you are not alone. It's likely that a majority of people have not discovered their purpose and I believe that is the primary reason for lack of fulfillment in life. Many are settling for less and working below their potential because of fear, financial insecurity, and ignorance of the prosperity laws.

The intelligence within you knows exactly what work will

bring you happiness, and your alignment with Universal Intelligence will bring you to it.

The great teacher Dr. Joseph Murphy once gave me words to stir up the forces of "right direction" on my behalf. Here are two versions . . .

Infinite Intelligence reveals to me my true place in life, where I am doing what I love to do, divinely happy and divinely prospered.

Infinite Intelligence opens up a new door of expression for me, where I am doing what I love to do, divinely happy and divinely prospered.

In the next section of this book, you will read inspiring stories of Feel Free to Prosper students who found their perfect work just from the application of the Lesson One material that you will be applying shortly.

I've got you covered!

*We were not given our unique talents
and abilities to earn a living.
They were given to us to create life.*

MARILYN JENETT
FEELFREETOPROSPER.COM

Attracting Ideal Clients

Attracting the Right Clients, Giving Up the Wrong Ones

I have found, through years of experience, that when we are not afraid of giving up the "lesser," the "greater" is right around the corner waiting to arrive. When I created my special event business, I was not only coordinating business events, I was also booking social events and weddings. I attracted a lot of wedding clients, but didn't enjoy dealing with that aspect of the business. At first, I was concerned about giving up that income. But when I finally became true to myself and honored my feelings, I released the fear and made the decision to no longer book wedding clients.

Almost immediately I attracted larger corporate and convention clients that were much more suited to my business personality and increased my income substantially. I learned that we will always gain when we follow our inner guidance. When we lose the fear and neediness, the right clients will gravitate to our business.

By applying prosperity techniques, we can also establish the dominant thought in our subconscious mind that we only attract those clients who are in perfect harmony with us.

If we adhere to these prosperity laws, our minds should not be focused on *getting* clients and increased business. When we focus instead on *having* clients and business, it stirs up the universal storehouse on our behalf.

Again, from the Feel Free to Prosper lesson material:

The subconscious mind will create for us and attract to us those circumstances that it accepts to be true in the present moment. That is its nature. It's compulsive. Our job is to condition our subconscious mind to accept what we want as if it's an **existing** reality.

If you will grasp this, your circumstances will change quickly. As long as you think and feel that you have to "get" clients, you are actually giving your subconscious mind the message that you don't have them now. And what your subconscious accepts . . . is what you get.

How would you feel right now if you had plenty of customers or clients? Happy . . . satisfied . . . grateful?

If you want to conjure up those feelings more easily, sit down and make a list of the qualities and attributes of your ideal clients. You don't need to create complete sentences, but if you do, make sure your phrasing is in present tense, as if you currently had those clients.

Divine Appointment

I often affirm and believe that the students and clients who are drawn to me come via divine appointment—they are meant to be my students and clients. We are drawn together for mutual benefit. Remember that what we focus on, we create, and that includes our ideal customers and clients.

When new clients contact you, don't mentally treat the communication as an inquiry. In my corporate business of two decades, when a client called, I assumed mentally and emotionally that they were mine and I always booked them. In the first conversation, I spoke as if they were already my client and began describing the proposal I would send them. I put my complete faith in the synchronicity that brought us together . . . *by divine appointment.*

36

Always Assume the Door Is Open

One of the most important lessons I teach my prosperity students is to **never** assume a door is closed based on outer appearances. Stated in the positive, **always** assume the door is open.

One of my private students experienced a wonderful example of this. Barbara was an attorney but, instead of continuing to practice law, she chose to work in attorney placement (recruiting).

She had a perfect candidate for a certain type of law firm and everything seemed to be completely synchronistic until the day she called to set up the appointment for her candidate's interview. When she called, the client informed her that they had decided to use another recruiting firm.

I explained to her that she must never assume that the door is closed—that anything can happen and she should not be "hypnotized" by appearances. Always leave the door open in your consciousness. Don't assume a result is final.

Well, only a week went by and the client called her to tell her that the other recruiting firm didn't work out after all, so they were still looking and needed her services. She called her candidate to make sure he was still available, and found out that he was. But again, when she called to arrange the interview, the client thanked her but told her they had just hired an attorney to fill the position. She congratulated the client and told him to feel free to call her in the future if they needed her help.

She was obviously disappointed but I reminded her again to always assume that the door is open. She bounced back.

A few days went by, and the client called her again. Apparently the attorney they hired did not accept the position after all.

By this time, she had come up with *two* perfect candidates for the firm and after all that had transpired, the preferred scenario would be for the client to decide which candidate to hire.

I was delighted when Barbara told me that she had consummated the placement for that firm. Delighted, but not surprised.

So you see, we must never consider an opportunity "lost" or gone. Based on our faith in the divine order of things, the Universe will create all manner of adjustments to bring to us what is rightfully ours. And often there must be adjustments in circumstances and timing to allow all of the right elements to come together perfectly in a situation.

The secret is to relax and trust.

It can make a profound difference in your ability to manifest.

You have everything to gain and nothing to lose from assuming that the door is open. You are in fact putting your trust in the divine instead of your own preconceived imaginings. But you have everything to lose if you push the door closed while it may just be ajar.

∼◠◠∼

37

Overcoming the Fear of Asking for Business

The first secret to getting over the fear of asking for business is this . . .

Fear comes from focus on the self—self-consciousness and self-involvement. Thoughts and emotions are centered on you.

So then . . . what we must do to overcome this fear is to shift our thinking to the other person—our potential customer or client. In our thoughts and emotions, we now change our focus to make it all about "them"—their needs, their goals, how we can be of help to benefit them. We hold the thought that we are providing a valuable service and product and wish to enhance the life experience of the other person.

Remember, it is an absolute fact that the mind cannot hold two opposing thoughts at the same time. And the thoughts we do hold consistently will eventually realize themselves as circumstances in our lives.

So it is of utmost importance that we deal with this issue of fear once and for all, and claim victory over it.

How can we do this? What is the final secret to our victory?

Earlier I mentioned one of my all-time favorite teachers and influences, Émile Coué. In the late 1800s and early 1900s, the

French psychologist and pharmacist taught us that the mind cannot accept two opposing thoughts at the same time, but a single thought will penetrate the subconscious and be acted upon.

The Coué method was to repeat autosuggestions early in the morning and prior to sleep, when the subconscious is most "fertile" and receptive to suggestion. Coué's patients experienced healings using his familiar suggestion, "Every day, in every way, I'm getting better and better," *Tous les jours à tous points de vue je vais de mieux en mieux*. When he toured America, his method became popular and was adopted by some of the most famous thinkers of our time.

Coué also taught us that when the imagination and will are in conflict, the imagination always wins. Therefore, what we imagine—what we dwell upon—will determine our circumstances and our actions. Our willpower alone cannot alter our situation. Instilling into our subconscious mind (imagination) the idea of what we desire will change our circumstances.

So, I ask . . .

What thoughts will you dwell on today and tomorrow? Fear? Confidence? Poise? That decision will determine your victory over fear.

How will it relate to this issue of asking for business?

If you remain centered and poised, but your prospective customer is not receptive, you can still remain confident that your mind and heart are in the right place—you really did intend to help them—and you carry on, knowing that you just had a valuable rehearsal. But you will be surprised to find that your outward focus on the other person, without attachment to the end result, will result in many more potential clients being receptive to your offerings.

38

~~~

Compete or Complete?

Imitation is the sincerest form of flattery.

It is important that we reach a point in our business where we understand the vast benefits of thinking creatively and not competitively. It's the point where we realize we are complete within ourselves and our business is supported and nurtured by the Universe. We only gain when we realize that there is enough for everyone and we wish the same for others that we wish for ourselves—and that means for our "competition," too.

Years ago, I had a major life lesson relating to this . . . as revealed in my entrepreneurial memoir . . .

When I created my business—the original idea of a location company for special events—I was considered a pioneer in the industry. My inspiration came from the film location companies which were very common in Los Angeles. But no one had ever thought of a location company for parties and events before. It was an entirely different industry, but I adopted the concept of location bookings from the established film location companies.

I may have imitated those companies but I didn't compete with them. My business had a unique twist—and that uniqueness brought me worldwide publicity. I sensed an opportunity—a missing link that had not been addressed—and I hit gold. I was guided to take an existing, established idea and make it different and better for another purpose.

On occasion I even used the services of the film location companies to secure certain venues when requirements were more extensive than for my typical bookings. We all profited from the collaboration.

> *If you can't say something nice . . . don't say nothin' at all.*
>
> —THUMPER, *Bambi* (1942)

At the time I created my business, there was a woman who owned a late film star's home in Beverly Hills. Although the home had the celebrity connotation, the "old Hollywood" décor did not appeal to my corporate clients, since there were many more beautiful mansions available to book. But I continued to show the home along with the others because I wanted to help the owner.

The owner eventually became upset because the clients wouldn't book the home. So she decided to become my only competitor and went for the business full force. We even ended up together in a feature story in the *Los Angeles Times*, in which we were depicted as "rivals." This occurred just a few years after I started my business. Prior to that time, I was the only "game" in town—and the only company of this kind in the world.

Now there was someone who openly copied my original concept, went after the same venues, some of the same clients, and even created a company name that started with one letter before mine in the alphabet, so that she would be listed above my company in the trade publications.

This was truly one of the greatest business and spiritual lessons of my life. Although it ruffled me quite a bit at first, I finally "lifted" myself above the situation. I realized that the competition was the best thing that ever could have happened to me and that in reality there was no competition. Those clients who were right for me easily found me. She attracted those who were right for her. It inspired me to be an even better businesswoman than I was and propelled me to new professionalism. It paid off. Her style of doing business was very different from mine. One of her specialties was weddings, which I stopped booking in favor of corporate clients. There were corporate clients who interviewed both of us but who contracted my services. I continued to wish her well and even sent her holiday cards on occasion. I was determined to stay spiritually on top of the situation. We occasionally spoke. I came to the realization that there is enough abundance for everyone in business and you can never lose what is rightfully yours except through fearful lack thinking and a negative consciousness. Lesson learned. It was a great growing experience toward my prosperity consciousness.

I don't believe in competition, at least in the traditional sense. Oh, sure, it may appear to be there on the surface, but when we focus on giving the very best of ourselves and rely on the universal source for our supply, we can trust that we will always be exactly where we are supposed to be with the right people and the right circumstances. We will be happy to afford others the same. If we feel threatened by competition, it only means one thing: We are operating from fear and lack and not from our true nature as children of a rich and abundant Universe.

We do not have to compete. We are complete. We are whole, complete, and perfect. When we recognize our completion within, all outer circumstances will be consummated, perfected, and completed to reflect our inner state.

If someone creates another business similar to yours, that's copying an idea. If you are the role model or primary influence, then you can be flattered.

What if someone copies us to the extent that there are violations or infringements? If they copy our quotes, text, or intellectual property without credit, then that's an infringement or "theft." We have the right to protect our interests and take action if needed—that's good business sense. But I like what the great teacher Dr. Joseph Murphy said: When you steal from your brother, you steal from yourself. What you wish for your brother, you wish for yourself. If someone does steal, the laws of their own mind and consciousness will take care of them.

The Universe doesn't miss a trick.

39

∽

Working Hard? Marilyn's Ol'
Book-a-Castle Trick

Someone asked: "If our thoughts had that much power, then why would we need to work so hard at our business? We could just create a mind thought for people to buy our services and products."

But you see, that is exactly the point! I'm sure you would agree that the majority of the population is working "hard" and not succeeding. There is an easier path to success. You can use the power of your mind—which connects you to the creative power of the Universe—to increase your business.

I would like to share a fascinating example from my special event business . . .

A booking for my corporate client, Campbell, was not going to be consummated. Campbell had come to me effortlessly—truly out of the blue—a couple of years before and I had secured locations for several of their national promotions targeted at children. This was the sixth promotion and we were at an impasse. I had found a castle in England that was perfect for the client's requirements. But the issue was with the timing of the promotion—the fulfillment date could not be moved up to accommodate the only week that the castle was available for us. But I knew in my heart of hearts that this castle was *the one*—the venue that was so perfect for this promotion. The specifics required for these promotions were so precise that finding the right venue was like finding the proverbial needle in a haystack.

For a couple of weeks, the client attempted to change the promotion date with their marketing department and ad agency, but they finally told me it was impossible. The planning for these multimillion-dollar promotions could not be altered and the date could not be changed. *End of discussion.* I had negotiated the price for the castle to perfectly accommodate the budget, but the available rental date just wouldn't work with the client's schedule. The client told me I would have to find another location.

Okay . . . time to go back to those creative forces. The Universe. The Quantum Field. The Field of All Possibilities. I don't care what you call it. I just know I can depend on it to come through for me. *End of discussion.* Hey, I've been practicing for decades and after you see it work over and over again, you just finally "get it." A request like this is elementary for the Universe.

So, I had a chat with the Universe. And the Universe told me to do exactly what I would teach my students to do. Of course! What technique might I teach a student to do in this situation? Got it!

I went right to the computer and prepared the contracts. For Campbell, there were two contracts along with an invoice for the deposit that were required to confirm a booking. I completed the contracts and prepared them for signature by Campbell, Eastnor Castle in England, and myself. I prepared the invoice for the deposit. I went to sleep. My job was done. It was time for the Universe to take over.

The next morning I received an urgent phone message and an

email from my contact at Campbell's marketing company. He said that that morning the client suddenly and inexplicably decided to go with the English castle after all and was changing the promotion date to start in February instead of May! The "impossible" happened. *My trust in the power of the Universe was greater than the power of a billion-dollar corporation!*

So please don't tell me about how hard we have to work. When I stopped working hard at my business, *that's* when it all starting flowing easily. The "hardest" thing is to release the belief that you have to work so hard, which may be the very thing that keeps you from your success. I remind you again of that little-known law, the law of reversed effort, which explains that the harder you try to do something, the less chance you have of achieving it.

And again, I am not suggesting that you take no action. What I *am* suggesting is that you take "inspired" action based on your intuitive guidance from the Universe—instead of working hard.

In Lesson One of Feel Free to Prosper, when I ask students to share their core belief about money and prosperity, do you know what one of the most common responses is? It's that they have to "work hard" and struggle to make money. Please recognize that belief for the lie that it is. Nurture your connection to your higher wisdom, your trust in universal guidance. You can learn and apply all of the great tools and tricks from the Universe's Marketing Manual.

Or . . . you can choose to work hard.

40

⌒⌒

Knowing When to Charge More
and to Charge Less

More and More

It was notable that when I started my business, I came up with a certain "minimum" profit I wanted to make. Within a very short time I didn't feel that profit was enough and I gingerly started to charge more. And then more. I kept stretching and kept raising my profit requirement.

Now, this is the most interesting part: The more I raised my prices, the more I attracted higher-paying clients. Each step forward helped me release the fear that I couldn't get more—or that maybe I wasn't worth more.

The caliber of client I attracted was directly related to the amount of profit I required for myself. The more I claimed for myself, the more the Universe brought me the clients who had the ability to pay and to accommodate my elevated prosperity consciousness. And the more I continued applying the prosperity principles, the more I claimed for myself.

Over time I completely eliminated the type of events that required much more work for much less money. I realize now that I was creating that "vacuum" for new, higher-paying clients to arrive. They kept arriving and new circumstances opened up to attract them.

The Universe will find a way to bring us the rewards that we claim for ourselves. But we must claim it—boldly—and know we deserve it. When we release the fear and doubt, the Universe will rush to support us.

We must make a decision. We are operating from integrity, we have a viable and valuable product or service to offer, there are plenty of clients or customers who will benefit from what we have to offer, and we deserve to be rewarded appropriately.

When Less Is More . . .

Okay, let's say you have reached a point where you know that you deserve to be rewarded fairly for your efforts and you charge accordingly. But there are certain times, if you let your intuition guide you, when you may feel prompted to provide your services for much less than your usual value. At those times you are "tuned in" and you may not know why you feel it is the right decision, but you just know and feel that it is. You don't think twice about it. These are times when you are being guided by that unseen hand— your higher self is directing you because there is more to the story than meets the eye.

A client, Michelin North America, was referred to me for a relatively small event. They were showcasing their new "designer" tires to the local auto industry with a reception at our city's automotive museum. They had invited only a few special guests, had already booked the museum so there was no profit for me there, and in short, there was a rather meager budget. The corporation, located in South Carolina (I'm in Los Angeles), didn't participate in conventions here, so there didn't seem to be much prospect for future business from them.

But my inner voice said, "Do it!" I coordinated the small event and gave it my best, the client expressed appreciation, and that was that.

A couple of months later I heard from the client again . . . they were planning to fly 250 of their best dealers from the East Coast to Los Angeles to celebrate New Year's Eve in grand style at the auto museum and to attend the Rose Parade, in which Michelin had a float. The celebration was commemorating the 100th Anniversary of Bibendum, the Michelin Man!

That New Year's Eve gala was a six-figure billing from my company, Marilyn Jenett Locations. And "Bib" was a big hit at his birthday party and on his float in the parade. He was also looking very buff for his age.

In the years following that event I coordinated other events in Los Angeles for Michelin. One was a huge media event that showcased ninety environmentally friendly cars, for which Édouard Michelin himself flew in from France. This is especially significant in that the event took place in October 2001, a month after the traumatic events of September 11, 2001.

It was generally known that following 9/11, the world turned upside down, and special events were canceled far and wide. People were not flying. Anthrax was major news. The hospitality and events industries were impacted greatly. But the Michelin media event, which was actually part of a three-day itinerary in three cities, went on as planned.

When we boldly claim our good, all of the forces of the Universe will come into play to fulfill our expectations, sometimes in the disguise of "little packages." When you listen to that inner voice . . . it will tell you when the little packages contain diamonds.

41

Can We Really Have
"the Universe on Speed Dial"?

"Who needs the Universe on speed dial when you have Marilyn?"
Susan posted on the Feel Free to Prosper Network:

> Marilyn always says that her program is like having
> the Universe on speed dial. I agree. But I found that
> having *Marilyn* on my speed dial (which she actually
> is—a bonus for being one of her select private students)
> is a **very** powerful thing!
>
> Yesterday I was in panic mode because the proposal
> I needed to move forward with a big design/development
> project for one of my newest clients was not delivered to
> me as promised—and the deadline was YESTERDAY! I
> couldn't reach the person creating the proposal and the
> whole project was riding on it.
>
> I called my back-up person but got no answer.
> Sometimes, this person can get very busy, so I thought I
> wouldn't hear from him and would be "up the creek."
> Yeah, I know, I know—that's negative thinking.
>
> That's why I called Marilyn for some much needed
> intervention for my negative thoughts and panicking
> mind. But she didn't answer. (She was actually on

another call at the time.) So, I left a voice mail and explained the situation and asked her to please call me with guidance.

I literally just hung up the phone after leaving the message, and lo and behold—my back-up person called. He was available for me immediately and was able to get a proposal to me in just a couple of short hours! I was soooo relieved!

I only needed to call Marilyn and leave a message . . . and everything worked itself out. Marilyn later explained that I didn't even need to speak to her. Speaking to her voice mail allowed our spirits to connect and help bring me back to the spiritual plane for guidance. And I certainly got it within **minutes**!

I just had to share my story. It was another lesson in the ways of the Universe.

The Wizard of Odds?

Let's discuss this subject . . . I think it's a very interesting one.

Perhaps I shouldn't take all the credit for this seemingly "supernatural" occurrence. Then again, I do believe I deserve more credit than the Wizard of Oz. Joking aside, you've heard me say that the "supernatural" is really quite natural once we understand the laws.

It appears that Susan recognized her connection with Spirit. I'll get back to her experience in a moment after I give you some background on the subject.

Many times in the past, students or potential students who have spoken to me have noticed that immediately after we connected, they would have a prosperity manifestation—sometimes before they received their program or lesson material. There are two reasons that a connection with a prosperity mentor or teacher can produce instant results.

Champion

One of my teachers was Champion K. Teutsch, Ph.D., an extraordinary man who was renowned for his groundbreaking work relating to mental and spiritual laws and consciousness. He was honored in many countries as well as in government, scientific, and medical circles. More than one movie star attributed their Academy Award to his mentoring. Government officials (even a presidential candidate) contacted him for help. He was truly one of a kind in this field and I was so fortunate that the Universe brought me to him.

Often when I went to Champion's office, he would tell me that as soon as I walked into his office, I would tune in to his consciousness. I would laugh about it in front of him. But then I would return to my office and a major piece of business would arrive out of the blue!

I was delighted by this but never really thought about it again over the years until I started teaching Feel Free to Prosper. The same thing would happen with my students or soon-to-be students—only in my case the contact was over the phone. Champion was again proven right, just as he had been proven right about many things in the medical and scientific communities.

We are all greatly affected and impacted by the consciousness of those around us. We have felt the influence of certain people who lifted us up or made us feel happy or joyous and we have sadly experienced the opposite effect of others. So it's not surprising to find that when we meet someone who has a prosperity conscious-ness and a firm faith and conviction in the laws, we can be influ-enced by and absorb their faith, vibration, or "frequency."

Susan's Wings

The other reason this happens is easy to understand once it's explained.

When a potential student resonates to me and we connect, they acquire new inspiration and hope—the possibility that they have found the answer and solution to their situation. What hap-pens then? Their subconscious mind immediately opens up with faith and expectation—and faith can move mountains (of negative thoughts and conditioning). Remember the biblical phrase about "faith as a grain of mustard seed"? Even the tiniest bit of faith when "sown" can open up our consciousness to grand manifestations.

We know that someone can be given a placebo (an inactive substance) instead of a medication and get the same positive results. What is that about? Faith.

Now, with regard to Susan's situation, she had been a student of mine for months and had experienced wonderful results. So I'd say that her faith level was high up on the scale. Yet some of her old worn-out patterns surfaced on occasion and she would get caught off guard when something would trigger this. But because of her prosperity work, her subconscious mind wanted to bring her back to her prosperity state. Her instinct was to reach out to her mentor, as this had worked for her in the past.

She would have found resolution if I spoke with her, but here is what I believe was happening with her at the time of that incident . . .

I have often stated that my definition of a mentor is someone who teaches their mentees to tap their own resources so that they don't need to depend on the mentor. The mentor teaches the eaglet to fly on its own. However, during the mentoring process, the student can lean on me and allow me to be the "bridge" to get there. They can rely on my faith in the laws until they have increased their own faith and conviction.

Susan was reaching out to Spirit—or Universal Mind—for guidance and help. I represented her connection to Spirit—her bridge. But in that instant of reaching out to Spirit, Spirit answered her. The longer walk and hand-holding by me across the bridge was no longer necessary.

Spirit wanted to reveal itself to her, and did a perfect job of doing so—even before she could reach me personally on the telephone. So I believe the eaglet was growing her wings and learning to fly on her own. Or we can say that Susan was discovering for herself what it's like to have the Universe on speed dial. Susan will then become a bridge for others in her life.

I hope this helps you understand the value of the right teacher or mentor to speed you to the consciousness and results that you desire. I'm honored that you are allowing me to guide *you* through this book.

42

Progression, Not Recession

I'm here to impact you with the truth of your being. Each of us has the innate ability to achieve victory no matter what is occurring in the outer world and despite popular opinion. All we need to do is to acquire wisdom and knowledge and apply it to prove this.

The first and most powerful thing you can do to become victorious during a downturn economy is . . .

Eliminate the word "recession" entirely from your vocabulary!

That's right. Stop saying it. Stop writing it. Stop feeding that message to your subconscious mind, which will only interpret it as an order. Stop mimicking mass mind thinking and media conversation. Forget the "R" word.

Who is the creative authority in your life? The mass mind? The media? Or is it the most powerful creative force in the Universe that responds to your words, thoughts, and feelings? (Choose one right now.)

Are you concerned about the economy and your business? The chapter entitled "The Single Most Immediate Thing You Can

Do—Right Now—to Increase Your Income" is worth reading again and again. Reinforcement is valuable and a key to prosperity consciousness.

Forget the "R" word. Stop referring to a "recession." Accept that there is no recession in *your* world. There is only progression in your life and in your business. Keep that thought firmly planted in your mind no matter what is happening in the outside world.

One of my favorite quotes is "One with God [the Universe] is a majority." Well, *you* are a progressive majority of one—with the great Mind of the Universe.

Even with the best of our efforts and intentions, there will always be situations that emerge that are beyond our control. Being beyond our control and remaining beyond our control are two different scenarios, as you are about to discover. Ultimately it depends upon where we will direct our focus. We have to choose whether we will align ourselves with mass mind thinking or take the path less traveled on our prosperity journey.

This story from my memoir should inspire you to keep thinking and speaking about your progression . . .

Out of Control

In 1992, the country was in recession, and I experienced my first exposure to a disaster and its effects—not only from a personal perspective, but through the eyes of an entrepreneur and business owner.

The Los Angeles riots, also known as the Rodney King riots, resulted from the acquittal of four police officers accused in the videotaped beating of Rodney King, a black motorist. Another reason cited for the uprising was the extremely high unemployment among residents of South Los Angeles, which had been hit very hard by the nationwide recession.

Viewers saw continuous television coverage of parts of our city in flames, lives lost and injured, and damage that was estimated up to $1 billion.

Obviously, many entertainment and sports events were postponed or canceled. You can imagine how the hospitality and special events industries are highly impacted by societal conditions and the economic climate. One large event that I coordinated that year went on as planned. But by 1993, I was definitely concentrating on the application of prosperity principles to create a surge of new business.

Cruise Control

During that time, while everyone in my industry was discussing how terrible business was, I refused to listen. Instead, I stuck my nose in my prosperity lessons and, without any other effort, a door opened that produced a miracle.

One day, out of the blue and for the first time, a saleswoman from the *Los Angeles Business Journal* called to ask if I would advertise in *Meetings & Conventions*—a supplement to the newspaper that would also be distributed to a couple of other major cities besides Los Angeles.

I told Eva, the saleswoman, that I never advertised (which was true), but suddenly my intuition prompted me to ask if they accepted articles from contributing writers. My own utterance surprised me. The truth is that I had never written an article in my life. Eva said I would need to speak to the editorial department to find out if I could submit an article to the appropriate editor. I recall that she was nice but not too encouraging. But I followed through. I was learning to pay serious attention to my intuitive promptings. The editorial department said I could submit an article, but there was no guarantee of acceptance.

I sat down to write an article relating to the wonderful event sites that Los Angeles had to offer the meeting planner. I painted word pictures of various Los Angeles locations without actually revealing names and I did my best to add intrigue and wit to my descriptions. I realized that this article could potentially be a draw to clients needing my services *if* it happened to be seen by those clients. I let my intuition guide me in the process. By now I was accustomed to asking for inner guidance and opening myself to receive it. But the foundation of my trust in this situation came from the fact that the phone call from Eva had arrived "out of the blue" as I was applying my prosperity techniques. I assumed that the Universe was responding to my need and I was meant to write this article.

I never mentioned my company name or myself in the article. But I did want to come across like I knew what I was talking about, so that the reader would assume that I really knew the business. My name and company were only mentioned in the byline at the end. In those days, we didn't have websites and links and the *Journal* didn't allow any contact information. The byline simply read:

Marilyn Jenett is the owner of Marilyn Jenett Locations, a renowned special event location company with offices in Los Angeles.

I titled the article "Unique Venues for Off-Site Events." The *Journal* published my article in the supplement and although I don't recall all the specific business that resulted from the exposure, there was one striking incident. A meeting planner located in Lake Success, New York (yes, that's the name of a village in Nassau County!), called and told me that she had been traveling and when she returned to her office, the supplement and my article were waiting on her desk! She was searching for venues to entertain doctor members for the Tenth World Congress of Gastroenterology to be held in Los Angeles—their first convention to be held in this city in forty-five years. I ultimately coordinated a large event for them at Universal Studios and a more intimate one in an Art Deco penthouse.

The business gained from that article—the first one I ever wrote—resulted in gross income to my company of $250,000! The profit wasn't bad either.

Walking the Talk—Revisiting My Roots

Want more proof of the results that can occur when you forget the "R" word and keep your attention focused on progression instead of the mass mind and media rhetoric? How about a more current manifestation to support these teachings?

As Feel Free to Prosper continued to grow, I gave up that last corporate client, Campbell Soup, after booking the over-the-top mansions, the English castle, and the private island for their huge promotions. It was time to devote myself exclusively to Feel Free to Prosper and to release my former business of two decades.

In 2008, our nation was in the throes of what was considered the worst economic downturn since the 1930s. As I advocated "progression, not recession" in my writings and interviews, two huge corporate clients came out of the blue and asked me to secure locations and coordinate their upscale events. I had no previous contact with these companies. I had not booked these types of events for five years. I was no longer involved with my events business and had no intention of seeking clients for that business. Moreover, all the news media were reporting serious cuts in corporate spending, especially for entertaining. The events industry was bemoaning a severe decrease in business. And yet I managed to attract two billion-dollar corporate clients even though I had released my business years before!

What does this mean? It means that if you maintain your prosperity thoughts and place your reliance exclusively on an abundant Universe that does not know scarcity or hard times, those who have money to spend will seek you out. But you must create the space in consciousness to receive them.

I accepted those two bookings because I felt that the Universe sent them to publicly support my conviction that with the right mindset, we can prosper in any economy. But following those bookings, I made the decision that I would never again coordinate events. I knew that my life had transitioned permanently and there was no turning back. My heart and soul would be exclusively devoted to helping others with my teachings.

The economy had not changed for *me*. What "R" word? I chose not to participate!

43

Positive or Negative Impact
on Your Business?

Our subject is still the economy. However, here are my nuts-and-bolts recommendations that will determine the impact that the economy will have on your business. Let's get down to business—and rise to your potential.

What Can I Be Thankful For?

Look at your business, your customers or clients, and pick out those things that you can truly be thankful for.

Focus on what's **right** about your business right now. Give thanks for those clients or customers that you **do** have. Don't focus on those who have tightened up their budgets or are missing in action—that may be temporary. And if not, start giving thanks for the new ones you are now attracting—yes, even before you attract them.

Gratitude is a most powerful way to become victorious over challenges that we feel we cannot control. We can control them—if we learn to answer to a higher authority.

Praise and Bless

Remember that what you praise and bless continues to grow and expand. This works for anything in your life. And now is the time to apply this principle to your business.

Here is one of the affirmations I used in my former events business when it was quiet and I wanted to manifest a new client:

I love my business and my business loves me.

Voilà! Within a very short time, a new corporate client would show up out of the blue. I believe my affirmation magnetized them right to my door.

Increase Your Trust Fund

Here is another set of affirmations to increase your trust and keep your attention focused where it belongs. I was once introduced to a woman who had achieved victory over a life-threatening form of leukemia five years prior to our meeting. Once, when I was experiencing a business upset, Marti called and got me right back on track with these affirmations. My situation was resolved the following day and produced even more profits than expected. I have used these to great reward and encourage my students—and you—to use them:

I can't wait to see what good comes from this!

*My **Trust** fund is enormous!*

Now, remember, it's not only the words of an affirmation that have the impact. It's the feeling attached to the words, so the more feeling you bring to an affirmation, the more effective it will be.

When things are slow in your business, you can cultivate the attitude of "I can't wait to see what good comes from this" or

"Only good can come from this" as the catalyst for guidance to other ideas for your business that can be even more productive or profitable than usual.

Loosen your "hold" on the habitual way of doing things and open yourself to new possibilities. We are creatures of habit and we know the subconscious mind does not want to change, so it often takes something uncomfortable to shake us up and out of a rut in order to grow.

You can use situations that appear to be negative to spring-board you into new and different avenues to prosper in your business and your life. You have absolutely nothing to lose by assuming the attitude that great possibilities await you, even when the rest of the nation or world is having a pity party.

Who Can I Serve?

Instead of constantly wondering how you can get more business, put your thoughts on what you can give, especially at a time like this.

"Who can I serve today?"

"What service can I provide right now that people need and will gladly pay for?"

If you have been following my other recommendations, your answers will surely come.

44

~

So What Is Real Success—to *You?*

I've had decades to ponder this idea of success and what it really means, and I have arrived at the following conclusion . . .

To me, success means being connected to your Universal Source of Supply—Invisible Substance—or whatever you perceive that creative intelligence to be. You know that with your connection in place, this source energy will provide you with whatever you require for your health, wealth, and happiness. Success is becoming open and receptive to receive your supply from the universal parent through the umbilical cord of your thoughts and feelings—through your belief.

Now, money, for example, can come and go. Someone can have a million dollars one day and lose it the next day in the stock market or in business. But the million dollars does not represent success. If a person is connected to their Source of supply, they know that Substance is unlimited and even though it may retreat, they know it will flow again toward them just like the tides. They know that Substance in any form, not just financial, is always available according to their ability to receive—according to their heartfelt, deep inner conviction and connection to the Source.

The late producer Mike Todd, one of Elizabeth Taylor's

husbands, said, "Being broke is a temporary situation. Being poor is a state of mind." Although I strongly suggest that you never use those "B" and "P" words, I have to say that this man truly had a success consciousness. He knew at some level, consciously or unconsciously, that appearances meant nothing and that he could always receive again because he was connected to his Source.

I have experienced outer success and accomplishment. I have also had my dark nights of the soul. But it was during one dark night of the soul—the final one—that I finally got it. I knew—really knew—that no matter what the appearance was at that moment, my supply was at hand because I was connected. Not just paying lip service, but really connected. My supply arrived, and it arrived faster than I ever could have imagined.

From that moment on, I have considered myself a success, no matter what the current condition of the "tides" was.

Years ago, one of my teachers gave me this affirmation:

All my wants and needs are filled now.

All my wants and needs are filled now. Perfect.

Knowing that whatever your need or want is, you have the ability to open your mind and heart to the Universe and receive it . . . without limitation . . . knowing that you are connected, tapped into the Source of every good thing, a Source that wants to give to you, not withhold from you . . . what could be more successful than that?

Success is not to be measured by how much material wealth is possessed, but whether you are able to create at will what you need.

—PARAMAHANSA YOGANANDA

45

How He Manifested a "Super" Role
in a Film . . . Literally

In November 2004, an entertainment news story in *USA Today* caught my attention. It was an extraordinary illustration of "playing the role" that we desire to become.

The young man in this story was a natural—he was unknowingly using the same principles taught in Feel Free to Prosper Lesson Three, "Accept It Now." As a result he manifested himself a super role in a movie. Literally. And in spite of some pretty tremendous odds.

Here's the inside scoop . . .

On Halloween 2003, Brandon walked into a Hollywood bowling alley in a very distinctive costume—glasses, dark suit, tie, and white shirt unbuttoned to reveal a blue undershirt with logo. Add the recognizable hair and it's no wonder he won first prize as Superman in their costume contest.

He had always wanted to play Superman and all his life people said he looked like Superman. But he was an unknown actor. On that Halloween night, though, Brandon *was* Superman.

Little did he know that a year later, after being chosen from thousands of international candidates, he would become the next

Man of Steel in a movie role that wasn't even a possibility that previous Halloween.

The name of the bowling alley was Lucky Strike, by the way. Was Brandon Routh just lucky? Of course not. We know better. It's not luck. It's law.

Accept It Now

Your acceptance of your desire in the now moment is your bridge that will take you from your present outer reality to your fulfilled desire. Words and affirmations are a great means to condition the subconscious mind to eliminate negative patterns and prepare for this advanced work. But I believe that one moment of acceptance of your desire, one moment filled with the reality of your answered prayer, is more powerful than a thousand affirmations stated without the corresponding feeling. That's because when we bring our feeling nature into play, we are imprinting directly on the subconscious mind and linking ourselves to the great creative forces of the Universe. It's like imprinting an image directly onto photographic film. Words and affirmations have their own important role because they help us to eliminate the mental debris so that we are able to access the film and produce an untarnished image.

—FROM FEEL FREE TO PROSPER LESSON THREE

46

❦

Formula for Becoming a Millionaire

I think this just may be the easiest formula in the world to manifest anything at all—profound in its effectiveness, brilliant in its simplicity. What do you think?

Many years ago, I saw a panel of self-made millionaires on a television program. At that time a million dollars was really a lot of money! Each of these people had started with absolutely nothing. For example, one woman's husband had left her with three children and no support and she borrowed $500 to start out. None of the panelists started with advantage.

There was one common denominator among the group, without exception. When the interviewer asked them what they would have done had things not worked out, the answer was always the same—the possibility never entered their minds.

Not one of them ever entertained the thought of failure.

It just never entered their minds.

Part Four

~

Feel Free to Prosper—
Inspiring Student Stories

Once it is recognized, once you become aware of that Presence and its responsiveness to you, you can never be the same. Once you learn to align yourself with the laws and that Presence, you have achieved Spiritual Intelligence—true intelligence.

—MARILYN

Feel Free to Prosper students are men and women from all walks of life and from across the globe—different backgrounds, financial situations, education, and cultures. They are business owners and employees, entrepreneurs, sales agents, professionals, working moms, job seekers, coaches, writers, artists, performers, students, retirees, and even an Olympic champion.

But they all have something very important in common. They share the one common denominator required for all prosperity students—they are *ready*. They are ready to change, ready to prosper, ready to move beyond limited thinking and beliefs into the potential they intuitively feel exists for them. They just need to be shown what to do.

I believe you are reading this right now because *you* are ready—you are reaching out to be shown what to do. So let the students on the following pages inspire you with their genuine and heartfelt accounts, for in the final section of this book, you are going to receive my most unique gift and be shown *exactly* what to do. I am going to give you the same lesson and mentoring session that first produced these student results.

Be prepared to become another Feel Free to Prosper success story. I can't wait to hear your good news.

*Feel Free to Prosper Student
Organizational Leadership*

~~~

Alison's Story

I was first introduced to Marilyn during a free Feel Free to Prosper online workshop. I was very intrigued by the mini-lessons and the postings of her students. I followed the students' posts to the Feel Free to Prosper Network and read about their incredible results with the lesson work. I remember posting a message to the network that I "couldn't afford" to join the new monthly program, but found it interesting. Marilyn instantly pointed out that I was creating that reality with my words.

At the time that I found Marilyn, I was at the lowest financial point of my life. As a recent immigrant to the U.S. with a young child, I had been unemployed for two years and my husband had been laid off from his job. There were times where we had to choose between paying the electric bill and buying groceries. I did not think that I had enough money to pay for the heating bill, let alone for Lesson One of the Feel Free to Prosper program.

I was still very intrigued by Marilyn's posted reply to me. I emailed her, and she said that if I committed to purchasing the program, she would email Lesson One to me and I could send the money in the mail at my convenience. I confirmed my commitment, began the lesson, and within 24 hours the manifestations started. I received more than I invested, much more. The most dramatic manifestations were forgiveness of a loan and a short-term nanny job that allowed me to watch our son while earning over $300 each weekend.

Within two months I sought Marilyn's help again as I was about to take my driver's license test. I had a phobia of driving and had not driven in over seven years. Marilyn gave me some affirmations, and I passed the driving test! The day after I passed the test I received a phone call for a job interview, and they wanted me to come in the next day. The job required driving (check) and was for career counseling disadvantaged or widowed/divorced women. They offered me the job on the spot and asked me to start the following day! Within one day I had a full-time job with salary and benefits, including health insurance (which we had not had in two years). Two months later I was able to purchase a new car (nicknamed Gladys, who has now accompanied me over 50,000 miles). The ability to drive again, and with confidence, was huge for me. Every time I get in the car I say, "Thank you for peace of mind and a safe journey."

Within six months the house across the street from us (from the apartment we were renting) was put on the market—a double-unit house for only $30,000. We were able to purchase the house and I became a first-time home owner. We are able to live in one unit while renting the other out, helping to offset the mortgage payment and home repairs. Our garden has been featured in the Garden Walk of Buffalo for the past two years and the living roof my husband created has been featured in local and national media. Also, there is a wonderful community of neighbors on our street.

A year into my job, I realized that the job environment was no longer the right fit for me and I felt it was time to find a new job.

I sought Marilyn's help, and she offered to mentor me privately. I had no idea where this money would come from. However, I trusted in Marilyn's teachings and I said "okay" with no idea of how I would pay her. A week later, I visited my dad, and he handed me a check for the exact amount out of the blue!

Then one day, while following Marilyn's guidance to manifest my ideal job, I felt guided to visit the website of a college that I had not visited before. Under job postings, they listed a job that was uniquely suited to my experience and background. Also, I dearly wished to return to graduate school, as my ultimate career dream is to become a professor. But I felt that it was too late for me to go back to school with a child to care for, financial obligations, etc. This job included health benefits for the family, with an added benefit of FREE TUITION for me and for family members! The job posting deadline had passed, so I thought it was too late, but my husband urged me to apply anyway and I sent in my résumé. A few weeks later, I received a call for an interview, and they offered me the job!

I am now happier in a position that I enjoy, with positive interpersonal relationships at work, and I am also twelve credits into my master's degree with a 4.0. The master's degree has another exciting component as well. The program has a study group format which applies to 40% of students' grades. The study group can be the most challenging or rewarding part of the program. I found a group of four other remarkable women and we have formed a cohesive, rewarding group. We are becoming an important part of each other's lives, and it is the best part of the education program so far. One of the members of the group stated that it was serendipitous for us to find each other, and our group name became "Serendipity" (Marilyn calls it "Synchronicity"). I should also note that a large part of this job is driving, too—when I think over the past few years, it's funny how everything lined up at the exact right time!

I am now enjoying my return to academia and feel I'm on the right path towards my goal of becoming a university professor. I will soon be applying to PhD programs.

ALISON WILCOX
Buffalo, NY

Update: I received my master's degree in April 2010—and again, returned for Marilyn's guidance to seek my next dream job. And I found it! I became a senior vice president for an organization empowering girls and young women. I love what I do, and the people that I work with. As an added bonus, my study group from my master's program created a side business—an organizational leadership consulting company. My annual income has more than doubled since I obtained my first job with Marilyn, and all this during a national recession!

I feel much more powerful now as I grow to understand more about the laws. I feel they have firmly "taken hold" in my subconscious and that I am truly able to create the life that I desire.

It's been wonderful going through this journey with Marilyn.

Feel Free to Prosper Student
Medical Doctor

~~~

Alexandra's Story

For nearly twenty years, I was an ob-gyn doctor in private practice in New York. Shortly before I met Marilyn, I decided that I would leave medicine and look for another business.

I first heard Marilyn on a conference call a few years ago and, although I can't recall now exactly what she said, I remember how her words spoke to me. I felt I had to telephone her right after that call and when she answered I said, "Marilyn, I need your help!"

I became a student of the Feel Free to Prosper program, studying the lessons and doing the homework. Immediately, remarkable things started to happen and unexpected money began to arrive. I got a telephone call stating I won a free gas card and, at a business conference in Las Vegas, I won hundreds of dollars in the slot machines in the first five minutes! Then during a session at a personal development seminar, the teacher was demonstrating a game with money and I obviously had the strongest intention to have the money because I won and went home $795 richer! These and many other seemingly inexplicable examples of increased prosperity continued to happen and it was certainly exciting!

It felt as though a slight shift in my thoughts could change everything. Of course I now understand the absolute truth of that, but after a lifetime of negative thinking, focusing on the positive and eliminating the old negativity was challenging. Being able to imagine and feel that what I wanted had already happened required some serious practice. However, Marilyn's lessons really helped me to overcome my old habits of worrying and, little by little, my thoughts and then my feelings shifted. I realized that in reality, a slight shift is enough to change everything!

When I decided to leave medicine, I wanted a business that would allow me to have a more balanced life—something that would bring a good income but also give me more time with my family. I tried several different home-based businesses but never seemed to find just the right one. Finally, I decided to study real estate investing and at an investment seminar I was introduced to a home-based business that was different than anything I had seen before. I got out Marilyn's lessons and studied them again and I began having excellent results right away. It was very easy to do and in my second week in that business I received a very substantial check!

Very recently, I used Marilyn's teachings to learn to trust and follow the Universe's guidance toward the right path—and it has been most exciting! I recently became a Florida resident, and I decided to apply for a Florida medical license because I felt that I still had a lot to contribute and I could favorably impact people as a physician. Marilyn always felt that my true calling was still in medicine. The process for medical licensure in Florida is fairly onerous and took about a year, and then I was required to appear before the Board of Medicine. Initially I was granted a license requiring direct supervision because I had had a significant six-year absence from practice. But then I was guided to the right attorney who had the board reconsider my case and they issued me an unrestricted license! This meant that I could choose to work as a physician in any number of different settings anywhere in the state of Florida!

I knew that I didn't want to practice ob-gyn again. I wanted more regular hours and didn't want the same life I had before. I was guided to search the Internet and I found the perfect opportunity where I joined an existing medical practice that was opening up a new location. My new partner is a fantastic person and now I have regular hours, no night calls, and the income is quite lucrative as well! And, I just closed my first real estate investment deal. The universal principles just keep on delivering for me and life just keeps getting better and better. Thanks, Marilyn!

ALEXANDRA TAYLOR, M.D.
Coral Springs, FL

~~~~~~~

Russ's Story

Marilyn's teachings have instilled a number of principles that continue to influence my life—gratitude, divine indifference, and one of my favorite sayings, "The universe is always on time."

Starting with Lesson One of her program, results began to appear almost immediately. I was going through a number of changes in my life, establishing a freelance web design business, selling my home, and dealing with relationship issues.

I was fortunate to have Marilyn's direct guidance during this time. She helped me with affirmations and visualization for receiving a price I wanted for my house—one that was higher than I had hoped for before starting her lessons. In fact, the house sold quickly for within $100 of that higher price. Not only did I attract a buyer, the universe had brought the RIGHT buyer for my home, with additional negotiations for appliances and the closing terms making it a unique and enjoyable experience.

My plan was to rent for three years until I knew what direction my business was going to take, and whether I would need the extra space demanded by a home-based venture.

As the closing date loomed nearer and nearer, I was unable to find a suitable rental property and expanded the search beyond my self-imposed price limit. My first viewing was of a loft in a small village on the north shore of Lake Erie. I immediately fell in love with the place—correction—I fell in love with the "space." It was perfect not only in size, but the layout, location, colors, and "feel" were inspiring for a creative freelancer like myself: 13-foot ceilings with an 18-foot vault, 28 feet of windows overlooking the harbor and Lake Erie, and an elevated rear deck and gazebo backing onto a marina. The only issue my mind struggled with was the price. I made an offer to the owner somewhere between his asking price and my original limit, then returned home and contacted Marilyn.

Again through her guidance and exercises, I went to bed that night knowing the loft was going to become my home. Early the next morning the owner called with a counter offer only $25 per month higher than my offer. Once again, not only was the price right, but the terms were ideal for my needs, including early access to the unit which helped make my move easy.

I had planned on buying new furniture but found that my budget didn't stretch as far as I had hoped. While driving to yet another furniture store, I was contemplating whether to go over my budget by $2,500 to purchase exactly what I wanted, or stick to my original budget and accept less in terms of quality and style. On that trip to the furniture store I received a call on my cell phone from a prospect from months earlier . . . and they were giving me a project worth $2,500. Talk about the Universe being on time!

Over these past few years I have returned to Lesson One several times and experienced results every time. I strive to make gratitude and divine indifference part of my daily habits. I continue to discover positive benefits in ways I could not have imagined when I first met Marilyn through an online networking website several years ago.

Part of the "magic of Marilyn" is the simplicity of the principles that she teaches. Rereading books or listening to audio programs that I have purchased over the past twenty-five years, I see now that the authors and speakers are talking about theories in harmony with these universal laws, or even making direct reference to them. But none of it "clicked" or began to influence my life until I came across Marilyn and committed to the deceptively simple exercises in her lessons.

Most recently I have used her principles to help achieve a weight loss of twenty-five pounds (and counting), and even to improve my pool game!

One important lesson was to not become attached to a specific item, person, or outcome, but to believe that what you need will be brought to you when you need it. For example, had I not secured the loft when I moved, the disappointment would be countered by the knowledge that the perfect home would come to me at the right time.

This understanding has helped me turn around situations that others may have considered major disappointments in life. A business partnership that I had spent several thousand dollars and almost a month working towards fell through at the very last moment. Was I disappointed? Absolutely . . . but I also knew that had it been the right deal at the right time, it would have closed. Two and a half years later I came to own that same business outright, and for considerably less than the partnership was going to cost. Not only was the Universe on time once again, it saved me tens of thousands of dollars in the process!

That belief system, the knowledge I now hold at the very core of my being, has even helped me in dealing with the end of a romantic relationship in my life.

Thanks to Marilyn's teachings, every day I awake knowing the right people, the right situations, and the right opportunities will come to me at the right time.

And that's a great way to live each day!

RUSS JACKMAN
Ontario, Canada

WWW.INTERNETADVISOR.CA

Catherine's Story

My name is Catherine Garceau, a passionate health advocate and Olympic medalist from Sydney 2000 in synchronized swimming. While my mission in life was revealed to me following a life changing experience I had while hiking the Red Rocks, getting out of my own way to make it happen created more struggle than I could handle . . .

You would think as an Olympic medalist, life is just made for you. The truth is that even someone with the drive and discipline to reach such an achievement in life can be just as vulnerable to life issues and a "dark night of the soul" as others—and sometimes more so.

My journey has been one of following my passion and interest to find the underlying causes behind disease, which for me was fueled by a need to free myself of disordered eating behaviors, depression, and anxiety. During this search, challenges always provided me with insight or new important information. At the same time, going against the wind often left me in a place of financial insecurity and scarcity.

At the dawn of my 31st birthday, I remember feeling upset,

and discouraged to *STILL* be living in a place of lack when, as everyone would always point out to me, I had so many potential channels for abundance to flow in. No matter what the reason, I couldn't get my mind around the fact that I had the knowledge and passion to create so much value for myself and others. I felt confused and doubtful about where to start. My challenge had always been to be way too hard on myself . . . it was now time to climb out of my own tailspin with regard to my health, body, and financial lack.

Just as I was reaching deep within, Marilyn Jenett and I met through unusual synchronicity. On our first conversation, I knew I had found the mentor/teacher I needed.

Marilyn's wisdom of the laws of the Universe and her own striking successes she attributes to synchronicity and guidance resonated with me very deeply, so I became a student of her Feel Free to Prosper program. Her approach was like no other I had studied before. She made it so simple that it became easy to apply the laws (unlike many other book philosophies I had tried to apply to my daily life).

The lessons and recordings of her audio program produced incredibly fast results.

In exactly two short weeks, I manifested a dream "home," job, and opportunity that was in perfect alignment with my vision—to bring my health goals and spiritual quest and outreach into action. It was the perfect environment to promote my own health and progress while also creating and developing special healing programs for others.

Over the years of doing the prosperity work with Marilyn, I have used Feel Free to Prosper to help uplift me through hard times. Every time, her work gives me a new level of appreciation for its simplicity and efficacy. I'm a much more confident woman because of it. My zest for life, resourcefulness, and intuition always get a spike when I use Marilyn's principles. I become more creative and financial avenues open up gracefully instead of with struggle.

I have often read and heard that prosperity in your bank account is nothing more than a reflection of your conscious and subconscious programming around money and prosperity. Change your mind, change your life. Easier said than done with our stubborn subconscious mind and unique emotional landscapes. Marilyn, however, helps us understand how to gently work with the subconscious so that it doesn't put up resistance, and allows for a peaceful shift into prosperity. I am a better wellness coach today, because I take into consideration this very principle (of not causing too much resistance) when I select affirmations for each person. My clients thank me for it, and I have Marilyn to thank.

Marilyn's work was a catalyst for a great shift in my life, which I continue to honor and be thankful for today. Magnetizing abundance in my life came from really understanding that the Source is ultimately the Universe, and that it IS unlimited. Going deeper and deeper by applying the lessons, I was able to change those feelings of separateness, poverty, and confusion to ones of complete Gratitude and Trust in the Universe's plan for me. Today, I see how I attract a reality that always matches my new feelings. If I don't like what I see, I know it's time to go back to the lessons and uncover another layer of abundance!

God, Spirit, Universe, or Source (whatever we choose to call it) is ALWAYS there waiting to be received into our lives, guide us, nurture us . . . and lead us in just the right direction, in the right place, or to the right people, no matter what is going on in our present reality.

Marilyn's own story of synchronicity and guidance and mastering universal laws has prepared her well to teach us to receive.

CATHERINE GARCEAU
Montreal, Canada

WWW.CATHERINEGARCEAU.COM

~~~~~~~~

Shondra's Story

My story is really one of going from suffering, lack, and limitation—living under the oppression of victimhood patterns—to that of freedom to fulfill my spiritual destiny of helping to heal a planet.

When I reached out and called Marilyn that day, my outer circumstances were dire, and I had only $5 of my own to work with, but I already knew it was necessary for me to dare to do what I could not yet see, if there was ever going to be something better for me and for my children. I had already rejected the "slow death sentence of the soul"—that would have been to just allow things to continue as they were.

I was a very dedicated, full-time, stay-at-home mom with four children ages eighteen months to thirteen years, and in a stress-filled marriage. Their father, controlling and abusive, had insufficiently addressed emotional/chemical imbalances that were very destructive to the family. It had snowballed to the point where I could no longer keep it together emotionally for everyone, with the constant strain of living on the edge of poverty and with no peace in the house. I was drained emotionally and energetically, just barely keeping the family and myself out of one crisis after another.

I also knew there was something important for me to do that was beyond the context of family, and that staying in such a vortex of negativity and lack would never allow me to get to it. Things HAD to change, and I had already come to the realization that I was never going to change *him*. I would have to make the change I needed to get myself and my four precious children out of the hole we were in.

It was a long shot when I asked Marilyn to help me for the only personal money I had—$5 in my PayPal account—promising to tithe the rest as I could. I remember feeling some shame that it was all I could offer, but even more, I remember the rising feeling of excitement when she agreed. I knew I had cracked open the door to my freedom. Because I felt so motivated to bring change to my life, I was diligent about applying the program she sent me. The first form of abundance that I remember was how it opened up love for me again. A beautiful, affirming online connection who briefly partnered with me in business jump-started my spiritual consulting and group work. That has grown to this day to include clients from about eighteen countries. Marilyn's program just seemed to work like magic as I applied it to my life, and money flowed in the wake of my full heart.

Within a few months, I was living on my own with the children, growing my confidence and personal income while functioning in my new role as a single working parent. By the end of the first year, I was living with the children in a different home in the country, rented completely on my own—without a man, a job, a regular income, or rent history of my own. Also, the Universe had literally gifted me with a great car with luxury features, one that I still drive today, three years later. An elderly man had died and left his car to "someone in need" and I was the one the Universe chose! I continued to step forward in faith, employing the prosperity work and watched in awe as our needs were being met.

Then came the point that I felt my spiritual path and work calling me to higher service and I realized that I could no longer continue as sole caregiver to all of the children and have enough time and focus to answer that call. The Universe responded magnificently as family members have become involved and their father has resolved many of his personal issues to help as well. I recently found out that the children's expenses and even higher education coverage is now being offered to them through an avenue that was totally unexpected. Meanwhile, I am freed up to pursue the important spiritual work I came to this planet to do.

For me, it is not about how much money I possess, or that I live a life of luxury. Rather, it is that I am abundantly provided for in my life and that my purpose on this planet is supported and fulfilled in the carrying out of my spiritual work and making my contribution to humanity.

When needs arise, funds and resources just rise to meet the occasion. Like a recent unexpected trip to Mexico for a seminar that cost several thousand dollars—within a week or so, the funds for the trip were completely covered. My new website is being constructed for a mere fraction of its potential $20K value. A professional service was lovingly rendered to me in a comfortable setting, at no charge, in exchange for work I had already done. A dynamic new love and healing work partner has shown up, available, and with all the qualities I specifically "ordered" from my Universe. Life is SO GOOD!

As I look at my progression from where I was when I began using the Feel Free to Prosper principles, I see how I was looking outside myself for emotional support, energetic sustenance, and financial maintenance—all things which, in my present (empowered) state, I now experience as completely provided from the Source within.

This is the grace of moving from an external economy focused on money (and fear of lack) to an internal economy of love and trust in ever-present abundance.

SHONDRA ~ ROSE OF LIGHT
West Virginia

WWW.ROSEOFLIGHT.COM

Michael's Story

Marilyn's teachings subtly influence events at Buckingham Palace . . .

Marilyn boldly states that with her teachings, you will have "the Universe on speed dial." Well that was interesting because I'd been getting used to the exact opposite—slowness.

In the first week of applying Marilyn's lessons, for a ghostwriting project, I confirmed a foreword by Prince Philip and a dedication by Lady Soames, daughter of Winston Churchill.

The Universe loves speed! Wow!!! The Palace response, almost immediately followed by Lady Soames's decision, was like a double sonic boom—a cosmic cry to me saying, "This stuff really works . . ."

A week later, the speed dial went crazy! I'd just finished writing my Feel Free to Prosper affirmations when there was a knock at the door. Manuscript back from the Palace with agreed foreword (brilliantly composed by Prince Philip). General rejoicing!

MICHAEL WARD
Copywriter/Ghostwriter

ISLE OF PORTLAND, UK

~~❦~~

Minerva's Story

My name is Minerva. I am a 24-year-old California Realtor and I am writing this with all my sincerity and gratitude. I have been working with Marilyn's prosperity program, and wanted to share the wonderful results I have seen, all within weeks of applying the lessons.

I have experienced amazing results, different and so much better than I had imagined, and I believe it is because of the simplicity of the first lesson material. I have closed three transactions, opened two new ones, and received many market analysis assignments from banks (which pay agents' fees). That's not all . . . I acquired four approved "ready-to-buy" buyers too. All of this since starting the lessons . . . and all of this is happening at the height of the 2009 economic recession in the U.S.

I was a little concerned about something at first. I wanted more income but did not want to take time away from my beautiful two-year-old son. Well, guess what? Since applying Marilyn's techniques in the first lesson I have manifested exactly what I affirmed. I always thought of success as the quote I once saw:

Success is being able to spend your time in your own way.

—ROBERT MORLEY

Since all this income has been coming in and I am attracting perfect business effortlessly, I have been able to save two whole days out of the week strictly for my son! I take him to the park, to the zoo, and we're creating so many wonderful memories, thoroughly enjoying the simple moments, and best of all, my entire mind is there with him! It's incredible, and everything I ever wanted. The best manifestation of all!

A couple of weeks later, as I was writing in my journal, listing all the unexpected opportunities and income, I looked at my list and thought, WOW! All of this within such a short time frame! I was getting ready to leave for a four-day training trip. Listen to all that happened before I left. An offer was accepted for one of my clients that I only took out twice. I received a counteroffer for another client. I funded on another transaction, which means it will close within days. I found out that all went well with inspections for another transaction, which will bring in a $2,500 bonus, and I got a referral from the same client.

I received three new market analysis assignments in one day—I usually get one or two assignments a week. I met with new referrals and got an email from an agent I referred a client to about six months ago. The client bought a house, it closed, and my referral check is on the way.

I then went shopping for new clothes which I hadn't done in a long time!

OK, that was right before I left . . .

When I came back only four days later, I had another client's offer accepted, two pre-approved buyers ready to begin their search, one successful close and another ready to close, two new escrows, a referral check, and a deposit in my account. All these great things were awaiting me. And the trip was wonderful, too, since my family came with me.

Ever since applying Marilyn's lesson work, I found myself with so much more spare time to do the things I love and enjoy. It's then that I realized how much time we can waste on worry and doubt, and trying to figure out in our heads how we are going to accomplish our goals. Not in my mind anymore . . . my mind is clear and peaceful and I trust that the higher power will provide me with what I need, when I need it, in an effortless way. With my spare time, I do crafts with my son, work on my scrapbooks, begin new projects, and just enjoy every moment of this life.

Another amazing manifestation once again put me in awe of the power we hold within. I was listening to Marilyn's audio session about creating the feeling state of having it now. I was right in the middle of the exercise, envisioning and feeling myself having these perfect clients and getting them into homes quickly and effortlessly. My mind was there, my heart was overflowing with joy, and then . . . the phone rang! I paused the audio and picked up the phone. It was a referral from a past client. Best kind of business an agent can hope for. He was ready to buy, fully approved, and wanted to meet as soon as possible. I set an appointment, and sat for a moment in silence before returning to Marilyn's lesson. I was amazed. Later that evening, the little old negative voice in my head started to return: "The market is so tough. It's going to be so hard to get him accepted in this market!" Well, I immediately replied, "Can't you see? The Universe sent me this client as a gift and not only is he going to be perfect, I will find him a home effortlessly." Against all odds, I took the client out only twice to see properties before we found his perfect home! Not only was it effortless, he truly is the perfect client. His family is so wonderful and appreciative and his daughters are precious.

So much to be grateful for, it makes my heart sing! I have dreamed of this moment. I am so happy, peaceful, grateful, and excited. Thank you, Marilyn. I have a new outlook on life.

MINERVA PANIAGUA
Real Estate Consultant

MANTECA, CA

~~~~~~

Poonam's Story

A degree from a prestigious U.S. university, experience working as a respected scientist in a multinational megacorporation, a dream house in a posh neighborhood, all the automobiles of my dreams, a happy family with kids and a loving husband—what a beautiful dream. But alas! The dreamer is a penniless, no basic education, no guidance kid of a bank employee bad-tempered father and housewife mother in a lower-class neighborhood.

That kid is now a grown-up adult and does have a degree from a reputable U.S. university, owns an aggressively growing multinational software company, has a beautiful dream house by the golf course, a loving husband that I chose, and two lovely kids. Life is full of comfort, beauty, and progress. I have confidence that I can attract anything at any time just with my thoughts.

From nothing to a comfortable stage did not happen overnight—it took over twenty-five years. But once I grasped the principles, it was almost instant results.

In my journey from a humble background as a small girl from Kanpur to one of an entrepreneur in international business, I realized that the maximum growth I ever experienced was when I had internal matters handily in place.

Let me tell you, I was not a born genius—I was not given any opportunity that I did not create. I grew up witnessing the pathetic condition of women in the social class in which I was born. Not much support, or money, or resources were available to me. But I learned that the principles that I applied to achieve something are universal. And that they can be mastered. They can be mastered and used at any time to create any desired results. When I was ready to receive, support came in many different forms and sources.

A constant drive to improve made me go over many books that have been published. Initially I was surprised to see that the things that went on inside my head before, during, and after the major breakthrough are the same things that are common in all achievers the world over. These are the same sets of universal laws that have been taught by most successful people and the oldest religions, like Hinduism, and they work without fail. It is just a matter of what religion or what teaching/learning method suits you. I found Feel Free to Prosper teaches the same things, but greatly simplified for a learner to easily grab hold of and understand . . .

Several years ago I cut two pictures from newspapers and put them in my journal. One was a picture of a golf course and another was a picture of a beautiful house with a grand entrance. I had heard that if you can see your dream it can come true and I wanted to have this grand house overlooking a golf course. Because my husband loves golf and he has always worked hard to make me smile, I wanted to have it as a gift to him. I told myself that one day I would have it.

Nothing happened for two years. Those pictures got misplaced. Then almost two years later I found them again and at the same time applied Marilyn's Feel Free to Prosper teachings. I looked at the photos, took a deep breath, and repeated to myself that this is my house and I am living there NOW. The next morning I went for my walk and imagined myself walking out of that house. I already knew it was my house.

My husband received a promotion at his job and I manifested new contracts for my IT services business. Less than two months later, I closed on my dream home overlooking one of the most prestigious golf courses.

I also had a fantastic "mind over matter" incident happen around the same time.

There is a very reputable, extremely rich person in India whom I wanted to meet. I knew him in his early teen years when he was without money, from a very poor family, and surrounded only by negatives.

I had forgotten all about him until about eighteen years later when I read about him in the news more and more. He is now a well-known figure in India.

I wondered . . . how . . . where . . . could I possibly meet him? I tried and tried to reach him. I made a trip to India and visited the city where he lived. But I could not reach him—he was just too busy and was surrounded by too many assistants and security. I came back to Chicago and thought to myself, "He is coming to meet me, with all the time in the world."

A month or so passed and he came to Seattle for business. He was on a six-day trip to the western part of the country only. He did not know where I lived on this earth and I doubted that he even remembered me. Without going into too much detail, one thing led to another and *he called me*. We spoke for hours, catching up on both of our journeys. He then canceled all of his appointments and trips to other destinations, rescheduled his international flight, and flew to Chicago to meet with me and my husband. This is what Marilyn refers to as "synchronicity."

Since that time, one of the oldest companies in India approached me and I have partnered with them in my IT business. They provide the infrastructure, manpower, and knowledge that have increased my business at least five to seven times over what it was previously, and the growth continues to be consistent.

My confidence is like a lion. I am a proven example that using these principles and consistent faith does produce desired results.

Marilyn, I am so glad to see that you have dedicated your life to people in giving them hope and tools to live happier and more fulfilling lives. It is indeed an open secret that one of the oldest religions has taught that the Universe is abundant. Abundant in all that is good and bad, desirable and undesirable . . . wanted and unwanted. One gets what one ASKS for, not what he or she meant to ask for.

There is a great emphasis on the power of the spoken word— Vani—in Hinduism. Vani simply means we attract what we speak. So we must be VERY careful in choosing the words that we use whether we mean it or not. Feel Free to Prosper teachings mirror that age-old wisdom.

Keep up the good work, Marilyn, and take it to more people who can benefit from Feel Free to Prosper.

POONAM GUPTA
Iyka Enterprises Inc.

CHICAGO, IL

Feel Free to Prosper Student
Healthcare Finance Professional

～❦～

Kevin's Story

My favorite holiday is Thanksgiving. You never know who will be at my house on Thanksgiving! Often people whom I haven't seen in years find themselves invited for Thanksgiving dinner— we've had an off-Broadway actor and a Minnesota Viking fan. I am always thankful for my friends and family and for our blessings, and I love to share my gratitude with those I know and care for.

Around Thanksgiving 2004, my friend introduced me to Feel Free to Prosper. Marilyn Jenett had a Gratitude conference call at that time and my friend thought I'd find it beneficial.

Well, the invitation to Marilyn's Gratitude Call has given me much to be thankful for. She has reminded me how much gratitude resonates within me. After the call I started to practice the things Marilyn discussed. Within a few weeks, wonderful things started to happen. First my real estate taxes were lowered, then my Federal Income Tax was lowered.

A couple of months later, in early 2005, I signed up for lessons and the Feel Free to Prosper program. And 2005 was a wonderfully prosperous year! After applying Marilyn's lessons, I received a promotion at work. Along with the promotion came a sizable salary increase—double digits! I received many offers and presents out of the blue that year. Then, just nine days into 2006, I received a payment from a business that included my principle investment plus 44% profit—just twenty-one days after I made the investment. As of 2009, while working far less hours, I've almost doubled my 2005 income despite the recent challenges faced in the economy, and I could very well surpass doubling my 2005 earnings. For all of this I am thankful to God, my family, friends, and Marilyn.

Marilyn, you and your prosperity lessons are wonderful. Thank you for helping make Thanksgiving last all year!

KEVIN HIGGINS
Houston, TX

Feel Free to Prosper Student
Ghostwriter/Literary Consultant

~~~

Claudia's Story

Feel Free to Prosper has completely transformed my life.

Back in 2006, I expected to break $100,000 for the first time in my life. Only missed it by a few thousand dollars. Life was good.

Then my husband got "constant-attention" sick and my business all but ceased to exist. Gone was my income, his paycheck, our savings, his 401(k) and profit sharing, our perfect credit rating . . . by the time we hit rock bottom, we owed the world and couldn't make payments. Creditors called constantly. We didn't even have the funds to declare bankruptcy.

Usually upbeat and positive, I lost my sense of "me" in the ongoing morass of our troubles. I was so negative I didn't care if I woke up in the morning. Finally, I tried something I'd forgotten about: I talked to the Universe, admitted I was out of ideas, and asked for help, any kind of help.

The very next day, Marilyn Jenett called.

It had suddenly come to her, she said, to get in touch with a mutual contact, who, during their conversation, mentioned that my husband and I were having a lot of trouble—maybe Marilyn could give us some help?

Can I say the rest is history? Because, oy, what a difference that phone call made!

In our first conversation, Marilyn pushed the right buttons to instantly dissipate my gloom. I had to get back to being me, to being that positive-energy force that always attracted clients!

I immediately began reading her program, writing out the homework, and, after the requisite week, listening to the recorded audio. Within days, my jazz-pianist husband landed a gig. Then more gigs. Soon he'd gone from one gig a week to four or five with new possibilities opening up everywhere. I was totally hooked.

Pretty soon I started getting results. A minor gig here. A slightly larger fee there. Before long I had clients calling and students enrolling in my Ghostwriting Certification classes. Mind-boggling.

Not long afterwards, when I got a referral to a high-ticket potential client, I knew it was a done deal even before we met!

I wasn't hoping—I knew that my subconscious manifests my future and I had programmed my subconscious using Marilyn's teachings and techniques. There was never any question. We signed a healthy contract at our second meeting—and I immediately bought the Feel Free to Prosper program as a gift for my dear friend and included Feel Free to Prosper in every one of my newsletters.

Because I know it works.

Because Marilyn has a piece of the truth that—despite her modesty—no one else has.

Because she has a way of putting the ease and logic in universal truths so that the "work" is effortless, the transformation is painless, and the manifestations are guaranteed.

My husband recently passed away, which brought additional

financial responsibilities. But again, synchronistically and right on time, another high-ticket client arrived, just the right person to work with during this sensitive period. My upcoming writing classes totally filled without effort on my part. I also asked the Universe, "What now?" and, through inspired action, founded my new publishing company, Iridescent Orange Press.

So in answer to those who keep asking me how I always have a steady stream of clients: This is how I do it. Marilyn's Feel Free to Prosper program has totally turned my life around and put me in control of my own destiny again.

Best investment I ever made. I'm back!

CLAUDIA SUZANNE
The Ghostwriting Expert
Tustin, CA

WWW.CLAUDIASUZANNE.COM

~~~

Bev's Story

When I first "met" Marilyn online in a social network forum, I was running in circles trying to find success with my art. All my life, like so many artists, I'd heard the phrase "starving artist," and all the sayings that went with it. "You'll never make a living at art," "You'll always need to keep your day job," and so on. My financial situation was dire, but I really wanted to work with Marilyn, so I took her posted comments to heart and simply trusted that something would work out. Within a week, I received a bequest from the estate of an elderly auntie, which was just enough to cover the cost of the Feel Free to Prosper program. Practically instant manifestation! Wow! I started to think that maybe Marilyn's state of mind was contagious!

Over the course of several months, I worked on the lessons and things began to improve. I got clearer about what I wanted to do with my art—animal portraiture—and I began to get commissions. I learned how to do better marketing and began to apply it to shows. As a result, I am better at closing sales, and have lost the fear of approaching strangers at shows. I take a few moments to see which paintings they are interested in, and then go and speak to them about it. Each piece I've done has a story attached to it, and it's the stories and the interaction with the artist that make the difference. People like to be able to say they know the artist, and I've learned that I'm not just selling my art—I'm selling myself as well.

I used to be such a naïf. I thought I wanted to sit quietly painting and let people come to me. The Universe led me to understand that what I needed was to learn to read people more effectively. Having that skill has benefited me immeasurably—not only in sales, but in successful relationships, both professional and personal. I have several really close friendships as a result, and those friendships are taking me in directions I might never have considered without having learned "people skills." Hanging out with other artists is a lot of fun, and lately I've even been going to a recording studio to help make a CD—even **more** fun!

I have also learned the value of PR and have developed good relationships with several journalists. I've become the "go-to per-son" when they want an artist's viewpoint or information about the local arts scene. This in turn results in more interviews and a higher profile. More exposure equals more sales, which means more income.

A couple of years after taking the Feel Free to Prosper pro-gram and changing my prosperity mindset, I manifested a trip to California where I had the great privilege of meeting Marilyn in person.

Now I am working on marketing and fundraising plans and initiatives with the provincial head office of the SPCA, and I recently purchased a large-format printer to handle my own work and that of other local artists—another income stream. I am also writing a book to help other artists learn what I've learned, and when it's published my income will take another big jump.

A lifelong dream of mine has been to create a strong sense of purpose within the scattered and disordered arts community in my area. Together with another artist, I started an arts council which quickly morphed into an arts foundation whose purpose was to create an arts center in my small town in Ontario. Approximately a year and a half after we defined our intention, an "angel" stepped forward to fund the center. We are about to purchase land and buildings and our center will be up and running shortly.

Marilyn taught me that it's not enough to dream. When you dream, you have to dream big—bigger than you ever thought possible. When you give your dreams full rein, the Universal Source steps in to make things happen in ways you never could have imagined. As human beings, we are limited to our human senses. The Source has no limitations. Trust it and let go.

BEV HANNA
Beverly J. Hanna Fine Art
Toronto, Canada

WWW.BEVHANNA.COM

Linda's Story

I've known Marilyn via the Internet and phone for a while. A phone conversation last fall ultimately led me out of a problem and to the right publisher for my latest book.

Since I've known Marilyn, most of my "aha!" moments have happened in connection with her—either after a conversation, email exchange . . . or "simply" going back to her teachings during a difficult set of circumstances.

I had four books on the market, but the fifth—*Reluctant Witness: Robert Taylor, Hollywood, & Communism*—held a special place in my heart. It was a book I'd worked on for fifteen years, dedicating much energy, time, money, and heart and soul to its creation. I felt as if I'd come to really know its subject, Golden Era movie star Robert Taylor, and it was as if I was telling the story of a father figure.

When Marilyn and I spoke that night, I'd just "lost" a publisher because of a lack of meeting of the minds, and I was a bit down. Marilyn, too, was working on a book. She had an agent and, though our books were different and our situations equally as different, we shared a common goal—finding a home for a work which, for both of us, came from our soul. This was deeply personal for both of us.

As mentioned, Marilyn has always been there when those "aha!" moments have come to me. This night, as we chatted on the phone, Marilyn said, "Let's manifest a publisher." I believe this was a Friday night.

I religiously repeated Marilyn's tailor-made affirmation for me that next day, Saturday. On Sunday, I attended the Baltimore Book Fair. I wasn't familiar with that part of town and knew only one person there. I was out of my comfort zone and I didn't think it would be a worthwhile use of my time. Things felt odd, but "something" told me I needed to be there, I needed to stay—so I did. I set up my table next to that one familiar person and we chatted as others entered the auditorium. By the time most were set up, there was one large table still unoccupied. It was only after the public started filtering in that the table's occupants came into the room. One woman stood out in front of, literally, an entourage. I eventually learned this woman was part of a publishing company.

The publishing company was predominantly a romance house and an "invitation only" publisher, which meant they didn't accept anything not solicited exclusively by them. I visited the table and talked with the woman, who was the publisher's marketing director, but she was also an author with her own cult following. She and her presentation were extraordinarily professional. I was impressed by the entire package. She asked what I wrote and I explained that I was predominantly a nonfiction author. I told her about my Robert Taylor book and problems with my previous publisher . . . saying I was now in the market for a new one.

Later that day, she stopped by my table to tell me she had called her publisher about my book. She encouraged me to submit to the company as they were branching out to nonfiction and I thanked her for making the effort on my behalf. Less than a week later, I did submit and, in short order, received notification that my book had been accepted for publication.

In less than forty-eight hours after working with Marilyn to find a publisher, the Universe had identified the right publisher. Within two weeks, I had signed a publishing contract. The project that I had been working on for so many years was put under contract almost immediately after I started working with Marilyn.

I haven't looked back since and I can see now that this publisher is so much better suited to not only this book, but to me and my work in general. I signed a multi-book contract with them and have two more books in the works. One is another biography, *Jack Kelly: A Maverick Life*—he was the star of television's *Maverick*—and the other a novel of "dark romantic suspense," which, as mentioned, is right up the publisher's alley.

I later built a promo campaign which nearly coincided with the 60th anniversary of Robert Taylor's appearance in front of the House Un-American Activities Committee and I enjoyed a cross-country book tour.

I'm a firm believer in Marilyn's take on the Universe. She has spent many years studying the Laws and how those Laws direct everything—literally everything that happens in life. If you let her, she will help you declutter your thinking so you can see, and feel, your true path in life . . . what seems like chance and coincidence will now become the joyous, delightful day-to-day uncovering of all that the Universe has in store for you!

Marilyn, you certainly teach all of us how to find that pipeline direct to the Divine! I thank God for sending you into my life . . . I've learned so much in the time we've known each other.

LINDA J. ALEXANDER
Frederick, MD

WWW.AUTHORSDEN.COM/LINDAALEXANDER

~~~~~~~

Paul and Sara's Story

Paul

My wife, Sara, and I launched both our businesses in the spring of 2007. I'm a photographer and Sara designs calligraphy, invitations, and beaded jewelry. A year later we both wanted to take our businesses to another level and asked Marilyn to mentor us.

We devoted ourselves to the mentoring and absorbed the lesson material right away. I even listened to the audios while I was running to train for a fund-raising marathon. It takes a little mental focus at first to switch your traditional thinking from "working hard" all the time to letting your life and business run smoothly with Marilyn's profound insight.

Marilyn and her teachings planted a seed that began blossoming into a big sturdy tree. The reputation for both our businesses has grown and we're becoming a strong brand name around town. This opened many doors to prosperity in our world. The Feel Free to Prosper program taught us how to think daily and how to receive more in our lives. Many of the following examples are "out of the blue" occurrences that were a direct result of this new thinking paradigm. Marilyn teaches her students how to receive. When

Sara and I ask for more business, more wealth, more clients, more accomplished goals and dreams, we are finally learning how to receive what we ask for.

Both Sara and I attracted more exposure and opportunities for our businesses. Sara's bridal clients and connections in the wedding industry increased, and other vendors became more aware of her services.

While mentoring us, Marilyn felt strongly about manifesting publicity for my "Big Yellow Bus" mobile photography studio. She insisted that my concept was a natural for media attention. Not long after that, completely out of the blue, I got a feature segment and live interview on our local CBS morning show!! The video is now on my website and is a great marketing tool. I've also been interviewed by the *Palm Beach Post* for a feature story.

Here are just some of the other results from Marilyn's teachings . . .

My photography business is constantly increasing—for weddings, families and children, and Bar and Bat Mitzvahs, proms, and other social events. But the increase in business clients has been especially significant. While doing Feel Free to Prosper "homework," I manifested a job for over ten offices throughout North and South Florida—an awesome project that took three weeks.

I learned that when one door closes, another opens—and it can even open two hours later and be more profitable than the first one. A company declined my proposal—the excuse was their budget. Two hours later I got a call out of the blue for dozens of executive headshots for over ten physicians' offices! Each day, I can't wait to see what's next in the big profit arena for me. It feels good to attract success.

There has been a noticeable increase in repeat business, which means people love our work and we have grateful clients.

Fund-raising organizations have partnered with our mobile photography studio for mutual profit. For example, this past Christmas, I took 5,000 "Santa" portraits in fourteen days. It's gratifying to realize that thousands of dollars have been transferred to charities as a result of my photography work.

Sara and I remind each other daily to be thankful for everything we are receiving and will receive. We're even more grateful for our friends, family, associates, and being able to contribute to important causes. We are also growing our dream of having foster care children in our home in the near future.

We are especially thankful for a closer marriage as a result of Marilyn's Feel Free to Prosper program. We communicate more, we are more in sync, and the "kiss and make up" part is much quicker now. This September is our 10th wedding anniversary.

We are grateful, Marilyn.

Sara

Before finding Marilyn and her Feel Free to Prosper program, both Paul and I had a passion for books. Not just any books, but books about success-minded individuals. After we got married, Paul and I combined our book collection to create a library in our home. Many of the books told us what to do, but Marilyn's teachings taught us how to think. Something clicked with her lessons and private guidance. Shortly after the mentoring phone sessions began, with Marilyn's mindset and our desire to advance our businesses and future together, results large and small trickled into our lives—especially "out of the blue" occurrences.

Paul's mobile studio photography business has grown with new social and business clients, including executive portraits for a major stock brokerage and for the physicians and staff of a major health care company.

Our ongoing work with the Office Depot Foundation, including Paul's "Santa" photos during the holidays, has not only created profits for us—it has also contributed substantial amounts of money to children and family charities, even during the country's extreme economic downturn.

I decided to give more wholehearted attention to my own invitation, calligraphy, and handcrafted jewelry business, so that Paul and I could diversify our income with both businesses. An industry professional with whom I had been in contact for two years suddenly started sending me referrals, which will be ongoing.

Paul and I will soon be celebrating our tenth wedding anniversary. Marilyn's teachings have also resulted in a closer, smoother relationship in our marriage. We are more in harmony, even while working together as a "team" in our businesses.

We learned that success is right in front of our noses! With the right mindset, the right teachings, the right focus, you can do it too. We are glad and grateful that Marilyn is the one who jumpstarted another spark for our future.

PAUL AND SARA FINKELSTEIN
Delray Beach, FL

WWW.PAULSTEVENPHOTOGRAPHY.COM

WWW.YOFIDESIGNS.COM

Feel Free to Prosper Students
Home Builder

~~~~~~~~

Valerie's Story

Something within me has always sensed that life is supposed to be easy and fun and that there must be a way to actually make this reality work. And yet with over thirty years of study in spiritual principles, energetic techniques, countless seminars, hundreds of self-help books, and even a degree in parapsychology . . . my search continued.

In addition to my spiritual pursuit . . .

My husband and I own a home-building company. At the start of Marilyn's program, we had close to a million dollars—all of our assets—invested in completed new homes sitting on the market. It had been eighteen months since our last home sale, which is a considerable length of time to go with no income. We needed a sale quickly or life as I had become accustomed to living could change radically. I was diligently using energetic techniques and principles I had learned to turn my financial situation around . . . but nothing was changing or happening.

. . . And then I came across Marilyn's Feel Free to Prosper program.

The basic principles of the program logically made sense to

me. And something inside of me was strongly directing me to try it. So I did.

Little did I know when I signed up for the program, the magic that was about to unfold. During the first ten days of the program, almost daily I have received something wonderful from the Universe—including unexpected dinner invitations, flowers, and compliments.

And then, a miracle happened. I got $843,400 in signed sales contracts, with an upcoming potential of an additional $300,000 sales contract the following week. And this was all within the first ten days of the program!

What occurred to me was, could this be the key to this reality I'd been searching for? Could it be that simple? After all my years of study and all the programs and techniques I had tried, was this actually the key to manifesting?

. . . I continued to follow Marilyn's program.

The next ten days of Marilyn's program were interesting. Most of the days were awesome with all kinds of wonderful things happening. But then I had a really bad day. I was angry and frustrated. I reread Marilyn's lessons and for the first time I had the tools to see myself through it. Previously, I never had a means to see myself through frustrating times and I'd give up. But this time was different. I realized through Marilyn's teachings that what was surfacing were past programs running in my head that I no longer had to accept as my current reality. I had a choice. I was being given the opportunity to rewire my subconscious mind and create a new reality. So, I applied the tools. And with that, the day that followed was magical.

I was staging one of our model homes for a home show and went on a shopping excursion with my daughter. The day was amazing. It was as if I had a magic genie watching over me, granting my every wish. I had front door parking at busy shopping centers. Everything I needed I found easily and most things were discounted. It was a wonderful, fun, and incredibly successful day. That night, I wrote thirty-seven things on my "good things that happened" list. I could have kept writing, but my hand got tired. So instead, I reread my list. And in so doing, what I realized was . . . my life had become magical, and magical was my new norm.

And it gets even better. With that acknowledgment I realized that the Universe has my back. The creative energy that exists is there for me, supporting me and giving me exactly what I ask for. And when this realization hit, it was amazing. I instantly knew that anything I want and anything I need—I've got it. I just need to get my conscious mind and my subconscious mind to agree on it. It's no longer . . . I wonder if it will happen. Now it's more . . . I can't wait to see how this one happens. And to know that and to feel that . . . *wow!*

. . . I have now been in the program for about six weeks.

My home sales have now reached $1,168,400. I have three more potential customers that upon closing will add $868,000 to that. Within one week from now, $234,000 of my financial obligations will be paid in full. And although the financial rewards of Marilyn's program are awesome and wonderful, what's most profound to me is that after all these years of searching, I believe I have found the key I've been looking for. Life can be easy and fun and Marilyn's easy and simple tools, when applied, actually make this reality work. Finally . . .

Thank you, Marilyn. I am truly grateful.

VALERIE PIOTROWSKI
Beverly Shores, IN

More Lesson One Results . . .

Renay . . .

I've heard many speakers being interviewed. I've listened to and studied the masters—Raymond Charles Barker, Dr. Murphy, Florence Scovel Shinn, Eckhart Tolle, Wallace Wattles, Napoleon Hill, the Fillmores—to name a few.

But . . . ten days ago my call to the Universe was answered after I listened to Marilyn Jenett speak on a show. Let me just say that the timing for this and the synchronization of her words with my soul were magical. She is that missing link that I've been searching for, the missing link to my manifestation of prosperity.

The simplicity of what she teaches and how it permeates the subconscious is putting my business on fire! I purchased her program. She said in two weeks you will begin to be prosperous. In ten days, the business I have currently under contract will generate close to $75,000!

I'm in week two, and this is so exciting to see what will happen next! I'm loving this new normal.

Marilyn . . . Thank you, Thank you, and Thank you for helping me put that piece together.

RENAY DANIELS
Bellingham, WA

WWW.BULLDOGBROKER.COM

Tina and LaMel . . .

Our house is saved!

Marilyn, I would like to thank you so much for your teaching!! The exercises that you had in your program worked out where we were able to save our house from foreclosure. We manifested $10,340.28 and were able to wire this money to our mortgage company!! I think the mortgage company was even shocked because every time we called them, they had to let us know that our house would be sold on 6/17/13.

Since we manifested the funds, I am now focused on our 25th wedding anniversary which is June 25! We have already priced some cruises to "Cozy Mel"!!

Thank you again for being such a great influence in our lives . . . Your teaching has been life-changing!!

LAMEL
Little Rock, AK

Good Morning Marilyn,

I'm ecstatic to report that LaMel's last message is *real*. Hallelujah, we had a breakthrough. We originally thought the mortgage company would accept our application for a modification of the loan, but it was denied. The old Tina would have started fretting, but thanks to your teaching, I was relaxed and was neutral and released the mortgage outcome to God. We received money from a couple of unexpected sources. We employed your techniques and used the tools you taught us to manifest our breakthrough.

Now on to the next thing—25th wedding anniversary vacation.

In the past, we have not enjoyed a vacation or celebration for any of our wedding anniversaries. Since next month marks the 25th silver anniversary year for us, we wanted to do something really exciting and memorable. We can't thank you enough, Marilyn.

In Gratitude,
TINA
Little Rock, AR

Update: It's now two years later. We still own our home in Arkansas, but we rented it to perfect tenants and it brings us additional income. Our family has moved to Nashville to start a new life.

Karen and Harry . . .

Hi Marilyn,

Three years ago my husband received a letter stating he owed $20,000 to the IRS. He was unemployed at the time this happened. He didn't file a couple of years, but we could not understand how they figured he owed $20,000. He was only a truck driver.

We knew we needed an attorney to help us, but we didn't have the money to hire one. We saw on the IRS site that they listed attorneys free of charge. So we got one and it's been a long road of court hearings, bank statements, paycheck stubs month after month (Harry's working now).

There was another hearing last month and they said that the final decision—whether they would take the offer the attorney presented or demand all of the money—was to be made in April (four months from now). They were waiting to see how much Harry made this year.

We ordered your Feel Free to Prosper program on Friday, December 14. My husband started the course on Sunday the 16th. I am writing this on Wednesday, December 19. Here it is just three days later and he received a call from his attorney today. After three years, the IRS realized they made a mistake and Harry only owes $700, which will be paid out of this year's refund, so nothing out-of-pocket.

$20,000 hanging over our heads to the IRS for three years and now we are free—just like that.

Thanks, Marilyn, for creating this program and sharing it with the world!

KAREN AND HARRY
Olathe, KS

Miranda . . .

Hello, Marilyn,

I wanted to tell you how grateful I am for your teachings and relay some of the amazing things that have happened since starting your program.

Before week one was over, I noticed an increase in my accounts online (I run an online business with several avenues of income). Also, in the first week, someone who has owed me money for eight years messaged me saying he'd left a check at my house (I wasn't home at the time). I got home and found a check for $2,000!!!! I had completely let go of that money, thinking I'd never see it again, and BOOM! It showed up right at my front door!!

This week, I checked one of my accounts, and as of today, I've had almost a 200 percent increase in income for this month. I can only imagine what the rest of the month will bring—not to mention the rest of my life!!

I'm *so* grateful for this program! It's completely changed the way I think about prosperity and many of my beliefs in just a few short weeks!

Thank you so much! I'm so grateful I was at the right place to receive this important message!

MIRANDA DOCKSTADER
St. George, UT

WWW.SASSYMOMPRENEUR.COM

Part Five

The Feel Free to Prosper®
Program—Legendary Lesson One

(Including Access to the Downloadable Audio Session)

If there is a secret, I believe it is that anything and everything we want is already there for us in Universal Mind, waiting for us to make a clear-cut decision and receive it through our powers of faith, belief, and acceptance.

—MARILYN

My flagship Feel Free to Prosper program is a unique lesson and mentoring experience that will change the course of your finances and life. Your consciousness can shift within a couple of weeks, possibly sooner, and you will attract opportunities and increase your income, not to mention the other areas of life that will be affected. This is a profound shift that can last a lifetime if you apply yourself and let me guide you.

The current version of the program consists of the digital lesson material along with my recorded interactive group mentoring. In this book, you will receive the printed lesson material for "legendary" Lesson One of the program, a link to the downloadable recording of the interactive group mentoring session based on the lesson, and printed highlights of the session.

The Feel Free to Prosper Program—Lesson One

The Feel Free to Prosper program begins with Lesson One, a powerful lesson that has traditionally produced results for my students—especially financial results—within two weeks. This is the lesson that brought floods of testimonials that established the credibility of the Feel Free to Prosper program, practically overnight. Shortly after I created Feel Free to Prosper in 2003, the value of the lessons became obvious as testimonials poured in, and the program quickly expanded into the complete two-month self-study format that it is today.

This is the lesson that starts it all . . . the lesson that my students apply immediately and that commonly results in prosperity manifestations *even before* listening to the first mentoring session. Lesson One has created miracles in thousands of lives over the years. The wonderful student stories that you have just read and that you will find on the Feel Free to Prosper website and social media sites are just a small sampling of my students' successes.

As a reader of this book, you are now going to receive the entire Lesson One printed in this book—the powerful lesson material and all related documents, including the highlights of the group mentoring session. You will also be given the link to access the downloadable recording of the companion group mentoring session. As you listen to the two-hour session, you'll experience more of my teachings as I interact with my students. You will feel like you are attending the live call.

Lesson One forms the foundation of the Feel Free to Prosper program and tills the soil of the mind to overcome the weeds of resistance—to easily and naturally grow a prosperity consciousness. The proprietary techniques in this lesson have never been shared with the public before. They have been reserved only for the students of my program. With this lesson and my guidance, you *will* bear fruit.

You will be given specific instructions to apply the lesson material for one week before listening to the audio session or reading the session highlights. It's important to **follow the directions exactly** for your greatest benefit.

The lesson "homework" does not take much time at all. You will spend about ten to fifteen minutes per day writing as I instruct, and the rest of the lesson will be absorbed in your mind as you go about your daily business. Your consciousness will be automatically changing to attract what you want, instead of what you don't want. Your subconscious mind will become your friend—aligned with your conscious desires instead of working against them.

How long will it take to get results? This first lesson is extremely effective and my average student experiences a shift and monetary results in less than two weeks, and many experience immediate results, even within days. For some students it may take longer, as we all have different backgrounds and experiences. But we're all made of the same mind stuff and the results will come as long as you persist. Here is your chance to learn and apply the most powerful prosperity principles available in a single lesson.

It's time to begin your two-week prosperity adventure. Let's go!

The Feel Free to Prosper Lesson One Material Included in This Book

Part 1:

Notes for New Feel Free to Prosper Students

What Actually Is Money?

Lesson One—The Spoken Word

Part 2:

Follow-Up to Lesson One

Marilyn's Moolah Magnetizer

Part 3:

Downloadable Recording of the Group Mentoring Session

Highlights of the Group Mentoring Session

Prosperity Meditation

New Feel Free to Prosper Student . . .

Welcome!

Please follow my step-by-step instructions **exactly** as I present them, and in the proper sequence. The program is divided into three parts. You will find instructions before each part.

Do not become impatient and move ahead more quickly than instructed. There is an important reason for the timing of the lesson material.

∼∼

Dear New Student:

Please note that this lesson material is my copyrighted intellectual property and cannot be reproduced in whole or in part, in any form or format, electronically or in print, without my express written permission.

Part 1

Please read *only* the following three sections at this time:

- Notes for New Feel Free to Prosper Students

- What Actually Is Money?

- Lesson One—The Spoken Word

Apply **Lesson One—The Spoken Word**—for <u>three or four days</u>. *Do not continue* to Part 2 until you have done this.

Notes for New Feel Free to Prosper Students

N_{ew} *Prosperity Student,*

Please read these notes before you begin the lessons that follow. You may refer to these notes at any time to help and encourage you while you are applying the lesson work.

Simplicity of Lesson

First, please do not be fooled by the simplistic appearance of the lesson. It may seem simple, but it is profoundly powerful. There are plenty of books and much information in the marketplace that approach the laws from an intellectual and philosophical standpoint. However, to get results, we must learn to apply the laws directly and incorporate them in our consciousness.

The subconscious responds to ideas that are simple and to the point. The advertising and marketing industries have known this for a long time. We are fertilizing the soil of your mind to prepare for planting, but we are also planting at the same time. When inspired to compose these lessons, I realized that the simplest approach and techniques would bring the fastest results.

The Affirmations

Please <u>do not change</u> any words in the affirmations of this first lesson. I have specially composed each affirmation and purposely used specific words that will not create resistance in the subconscious. If you change even one word, it may prevent you from getting the intended results. So don't get creative at this time—follow my instructions to the letter.

Exception: If English is not your native language, then you may translate the words into your mother tongue. I believe this will help the subconscious accept them. You may also use both languages.

When I had Lesson One translated into another language years ago, I had an excellent translator who explained that sometimes the literal translation of a word may not have the same meaning. So she was careful to translate all words into the true meaning I intended.

Skipping a Day of Writing

Do not feel "guilty" if you skip a day or two of writing your affirmations. That is counterproductive—feeling guilty, that is. It's fine to skip a day if you must, just pick up again the next day. But don't skip too much time during this initial period.

Do Not Force—Easy Does It

It is also important that you do not "force" this work. Easy does it. It's the steady input of information, the repetition, that will do the job, but relax about it. If you are relaxed, your mind gets the message that what you are writing is a reality. If you are tense, you are telling your mind the opposite.

Writer's Cramp?

Complaints about writer's cramp? Well, regarding the written homework, I always tell my students that you are using prosperity muscles that you haven't used before. A small price to pay for success, don't you think? You may break up your writing session if it's more comfortable—maybe write ten affirmations at a time and at different times. Again, what's important is the steady input into the mind. The fact is that handwriting greatly impacts the subconscious mind, more than typing, so my instructions aren't frivolous.

Here's the "proof" I manifested that should motivate you—the proof that handwriting trumps typing and the reason why writing affirmations impacts the brain to create results. University researchers in Norway and France finally provided the scientific evidence that I had been seeking since I began teaching Feel Free to Prosper in 2003. From *Bloomberg Businessweek* . . .

Pen Mightier Than Keyboard for
Making Imprint on Brain
www.feelfreetoprosper.com/pen

The only excuse would be if you have a physical disability, in which case you will find the best alternatives to handwriting at this link: www.feelfreetoprosper.com/writing.

Do keep at it. The second week is an important time and it's when most of my students experience a shift and start manifesting. This seemingly mundane work will pay off. And the audio mentoring session will bring a whole new aspect to it.

Don't Deny What You Affirm

As you continue applying the lesson, your subconscious will begin to shift and will become your friend. It will alert you when you are making negative statements because they are not aligned with the new ideas that you are planting. You'll find that you are "catching yourself" at these times, where in the past you didn't pay attention. This is a good indication of your shifting consciousness.

Do make an effort, however, to stop your negative thoughts and words as they appear. Immediately—before you even finish the negative thought or statement—turn it around and replace it with the opposite: a positive statement, or with the lesson words "wealth success." Your attention to this will greatly speed up your progress.

Other Signs

Other signs that indicate that your subconscious is absorbing the lesson material are: You will begin to feel lighter physically and mentally. It is almost as if, literally, a burden is being lifted. You will feel more positive and hopeful about your life situations. You will become more aware that solutions, results, and prosperity **are** possible. You will feel a confidence that you didn't have before. Many of these signs will appear even **before** you manifest any outer tangible results. It is the inner that produces the outer. Your "inner world" is preparing you for outer results.

Apparent Setbacks While Doing This Work

These "appearances" are the aftermath—the effect—of previous lack thoughts and beliefs—the cause. You must "weather the storm" and ride with it. All of these new thoughts and ideas that you are instilling in your mind will result in new circumstances and conditions. So do not be alarmed by this, and don't give up!

Panic, anxiety, nervousness, and impatience will keep your results away. When the outer appearances don't upset you and you can remain calm and neutral in spite of them, that's when results come.

"This too shall pass" is an excellent reminder. Relax as best you can to release the fear. If you live in gratitude for all the good things, those other situations will resolve themselves.

Keep planting new seeds, and flowers will replace the weeds. We live in a time/space world and a certain amount of time elapses between the cause and its effect. So you are experiencing the effects of the old way of thinking. Soon you will experience the effects of the new way. Perseverance is the key.

Reading or Applying Other Prosperity Material

I highly recommend that students of the Feel Free to Prosper program **do not** apply other material and programs relating to this subject—universal laws, prosperity principles, and mental or subconscious techniques—while you are doing this lesson work. That includes even the wonderful books and programs that are available and the teachers and books I mention in my classes. The subconscious mind responds to simplicity. There will be plenty of time to read, explore, and research later on.

If you are purchasing other programs at the same time, please either apply the other programs before mine or wait until you have finished the Feel Free to Prosper lessons.

There is a very good reason for this. Again, when I was first guided to compose and offer this program, I asked the Universe how I could present these principles in a way that others could grasp easily and not have to go through the thirty-year journey that I did. I intuitively knew that there were two distinct issues that needed to be addressed: overload and confusion.

In order to get the best and fastest results, we must not overload the subconscious mind and we must not confuse it. So a clear, precise, simple approach without interference that may confuse or complicate is what this lesson work requires—in the initial stages of breaking through into a new consciousness.

In my lessons, I often refer to great teachers and their works. However, I still recommend that my students not read the works of those teachers while applying my lessons.

Prosperity Scientist

You are a scientist performing a life-changing experiment in the laboratory of your mind. You are "brewing" a new consciousness. It is important to have just the proper amount of ingredients. It is important not to allow contaminants to enter your laboratory or your mental brew. You are on your way to brilliant success, for you have the greatest power in the Universe as your benefactor.

What Actually Is Money?

I once asked the question: What actually is money? I waited until everyone provided responses, and then offered mine. Here is my definition of money, through the words of Charles Fillmore, cofounder of the Unity spiritual movement.

Spiritual Substance—The Fundamental Basis of the Universe

The spiritual substance from which comes all visible wealth is never depleted. It is right with you all the time and responds to your faith in it and your demands on it. It is not affected by our ignorant talk of hard times, though *we* are affected because our thoughts and words govern our demonstration. The unfailing resource is always ready to give. It has no choice in the matter; it must give, for that is its nature. Pour your living words of faith into the omnipresent substance, and you will be prospered though all the banks in the world close their doors. Turn the great energy of your thinking toward "plenty" ideas, and you will have plenty regardless of what men about you are saying or doing.

There is no scarcity of the air you breathe. There is plenty of air, all you will ever need, but if you close your lungs and refuse to breathe, you will not get it and may suffocate for lack of air. When you recognize the presence of abundance of air and open your lungs to breathe it deeply, you get a larger inspiration. This is exactly what you should do with your mind in regard to substance. There is an all-sufficiency of all things, just as there is an all-sufficiency of air. The only lack is our own lack of appropriation.

The spiritual substance is steadfast and immovable, enduring. It does not fluctuate with market reports. It does not decrease in "hard times" nor increase in "good times." It cannot be hoarded away to cause a deficiency in supply and a higher price. It cannot be exhausted in doles to meet the needs of privation. It is ever the same, constant, abundant, freely circulating and available.

All manifest substance flows from the realm of light waves, according to the findings of modern physical science. One or more light particles, electrons, form the atom that is the basis of all physical manifestation.

Man must build a perfect soul structure with faculties capable of always producing abundantly for both his spiritual and his material welfare. In order to accomplish this, man must become familiar with what the metaphysician terms omnipresent Spirit substance, which is visible only to mind and the nature of which is to sustain and enrich whatever idea is projected into it.

This Spirit substance stands back of and gives support to man's every thought and word. It is ready to provide food for all living creatures everywhere.

Today man is learning consciously to make union with this invisible spiritual thought stuff and appropriate and manifest it. Our supply and support is governed by our familiarity with substance and by our mental hold upon it. Spiritual substance is the source of all material wealth and cannot suffer loss or destruction by human thought. It is always with us, ready to be used and to make potent and fertile both the soul and the body consciousness.

Just as the earth is the universal matrix in which all vegetation develops so this invisible Spirit substance is the universal matrix in which ideas of prosperity germinate and grow and bring forth according to our faith and trust.

If we are to go forward spiritually, we must not waste our thought stuff in idle thoughts, in thinking thoughts of poverty, discontent, jealousy. We should positively weed out of consciousness all thoughts of poverty and failure, and in thinking or speaking of our affairs we should use the very highest and best language at our command.

Whatever the seed word is that is implanted in omnipresent Spirit substance, this seed word will germinate and grow and bring forth fruit "after its kind." Just as the farmer therefore selects the very best seed corn for planting, so we must choose the words that will bring forth the rich harvest of plenty.

To gain control of Spirit substance we grasp it with our mind; that is, lay hold of the idea back of it. Right thinking is necessary in using the mind constructively to bring about right results.*

---

* Charles Fillmore, excerpts from *Prosperity* and *Teach Us to Pray.* Used with permission of Unity, www.unity.org.

Lesson One—The Spoken Word

Introduction

In this program, I am going to share with you simple but vastly underused techniques that can greatly impact your income, business, or career, and can in fact change all aspects of your life for the better. The principles are sound and based on ageless wisdom, so I will avoid detailed intellectual discussion. I ask only that you have an open mind and a basic faith in the working of your mind based on what you are about to learn.

If you use the techniques and put them to the test, you will get results. This will increase your confidence in the ability of your mind to create and attract what you want, and you will have an inner peace in knowing that you do have control over your circumstances, that you are indeed the master of your fate.

Dual Nature of Mind

Most of us know that we have a conscious mind and a subconscious mind. The conscious mind reasons and deduces. The subconscious mind is the storehouse of total memory, the seed of habit, the seat of intuition, and for our purposes here, the faithful servant that takes "orders" from the conscious mind.

The subconscious accepts suggestion through the spoken word, inner thoughts, and outside influences. Once impregnated with a suggestion, it will automatically and compulsively act on that idea to manifest the end result. The subconscious does not have the ability to make judgments and does not reason whether this result is positive or negative—it merely acts on the given command to ensure its fulfillment. The same neutral mental power that produces good in your life also produces that which is not good. Just like electricity, it can be used as a great power for good or a great force for destruction.

The Spoken Word

Every word we speak, every thought we think, and every emotion we feel is recorded in the subconscious. Through repetition, or with enough faith or emotional impact, the subconscious will accept our words as a command and will create subjectively and also attract and magnetize circumstances, conditions, and persons to ensure the manifestation of our "order."

Even words spoken casually can bypass the conscious mind and drop into the subconscious and take root. It has been said, "The subconscious mind cannot take a joke." Seemingly harmless expressions, if accepted by the subconscious, can produce undesirable results in our lives.

Something to think about

How many times today have you said aloud or to yourself, even casually, "I can't afford . . ."

On the other hand, positive, life-enhancing, prosperous, success-oriented words will produce results that correspond and can bring about astonishing results and turn situations around dramatically. Repeating successful, prospering words will ensure success and prosperity in your work, in your business, in your career or professional life. The repetition of prospering words will open up the channels for income from both expected and unexpected sources.

My experience

Over the years, I have attracted several unexpected opportunities that were totally unrelated to my business and, in fact, these were situations that had never presented themselves before and in which I had no previous experience.

Did they just come out of the blue? They most certainly did. My definition of the "blue" is that vast Universe with infinite possibilities, which will offer its gifts if we will just open and prepare our minds to receive. I considered each of these opportunities such a gift and decided right then and there that each was meant for me as a channel for income. I succeeded at each of these endeavors and created thousands of dollars in unexpected income.

The subconscious mind acts on the *dominant* thought therein. The repetition of positive words will eventually replace negative patterns in the subconscious, which block our success and limit our income and our good.

If we persist in adding clean water, drop by drop, into a bucket of muddy water, eventually we will end up with a bucket of clean water. The good news is that we don't need to completely fill our mind bucket—the dominant thought is all that is necessary for the subconscious to respond and create our desired result. So we don't have to completely eliminate the negative thoughts. Fifty-one percent positive, and we get the golden ring.

I know you are asking, "How long will this take?" I believe it will depend upon how diligently you apply the techniques and use positive words. And just as importantly, how carefully you monitor yourself so that you don't counteract the good mental work you are doing. One great teacher said that if you asked a taxi driver to take you somewhere but gave him two addresses, where would you end up? Certainly not at your destination. So if your destination is increased income, don't give your subconscious taxi two different directions!

It's vitally important to monitor the words we say. We must become aware of the impact of the words we are saying and thinking (self-talk is just as powerful), as these words create our intent, our mood, our ability to attract and repel, the story and very fabric of our lives (I do get dramatic at times).

Something to think about

What if you had a genie with you every moment of your life and this genie would give you anything you wanted, anything you asked for, and all you had to do was say the word? That's right—just say the word and it was yours. What words would you be saying? That genie is your subconscious mind.

So now you are going to choose carefully your words, especially the words that you attach to "I" or "I am." From this moment on, when someone asks, "How are you?" or "How's it going?" or "How's the career?"—no matter what has been transpiring, just respond, "Fantastic!" or "Great!" or "Getting better all the time!" and see how quickly your life will evolve to accommodate your new orders.

"Aren't we lying when we do this?" I hear you asking. Of

course not. I am not teaching a course on lying. We are acting "as if." Yes, we are acting. Like Hollywood actors, we are acting upon that great "screen" of our subconscious, playing the role, impressing our desire on the inner celluloid, and, once impressed, our desire will appear in our outer world, at a premier, for all to see.

Act as though I am, and I will be. Think about, bring about. As within, so without. Fake it till you make it.

Homework!

1. Study Lesson One. Read it several times. Don't just think about it, absorb it and feel its meaning.

2. Here are two words that you are to say several times a day, for several minutes. The subconscious mind is very open to suggestion when we are in the relaxed alpha state—upon falling asleep and when we awaken. These are excellent times to repeat these words. But also repeat them during the day. They are wonderful words to say whenever you have a negative thought about your finances. Immediately stop the thought by repeating these words. Immediately substitute the negative thoughts and words with these positive ones. The words are:

Wealth, Success   Wealth, Success   Wealth, Success

The repetition of these words will start to create the feeling of wealth and success within you. There is a reason I am having you just say the words and not turn them into an "affirmation." By just saying the words, you are not creating an argument in the subconscious with regard to finances.

3. There *is* an affirmation I am going to give you at this time. This particular one is going to speed up your progress and also prepare you for future lessons if you choose to continue with the Feel Free to Prosper program beyond this book. Every day until Part 2, write this affirmation by hand twenty-five times:

I easily accept new prosperity thoughts and I am prepared to increase my income now.

4. Okay, get ready for this one. This is big. But if you want to get results sooner rather than later, you need to do this. This is not for the fainthearted.

For this lesson period (I really mean forever, but I'm trying to be gentle), you will not make another negative statement about your finances. Repeat . . . **No Negative Statements About Your Finances**. No negative words regarding money. No conversation with your family, friends, lover, pet, business associates, strangers, creditors, extraterrestrials, etc. For the entire lesson period, you are to make **Only Positive Statements** to anyone about your finances. Including to yourself.

(Just be thankful I didn't say that you are to have no negative *thoughts* about your finances! That will naturally follow in time.)

I hope you realize what this means. It means that if you have loved ones or friends or associates who are constantly speaking negatively about money, you will need to avoid them or you will need to tell them, and mean it, that you will not engage in any negative conversation. Period. If you want to attract money, there is a price to pay. That price is a total shift in consciousness. That is what we are doing now.

5. Keep notes or a journal and every night write down in a brief list all the good things that happened to you that day. Make a note of all income but pay particular attention to **unexpected** income. This learning process will open the channels for income and opportunities to flow to you from sometimes very surprising sources. When an opportunity, client, or job appears, even if you will actually be paid a bit later, still write that entry as unexpected income. There is more to learn about gratitude in the Feel Free to Prosper teachings, but for now, give thanks to the Universe for all of the good that has come to you that day.

Part 2

Have you applied the previous Lesson One homework for three or four days? If so, you may now move on to Part Two and these sections:

- Follow-Up to Lesson One

- Marilyn's Moolah Magnetizer

Apply the Follow-up to Lesson One for <u>the remainder of the week</u> and substitute the new affirmation in this section for the previous one. The Moolah Magnetizer will reinforce the homework you have been doing. I believe you will find this calming and very uplifting with regard to money, but please don't think it's not powerful. It is . . . the subconscious mind accepts this visual literally and translates it to outer circumstances. So enjoy Marilyn's Moolah Magnetizer, my own creation. I had used this myself in the past, but never put it to words before creating the program.

Are you continuing to write your affirmations? As you know by now, I'm adamant about the benefits of handwriting them. Still need more encouragement to keep doing it? This should help . . .

A Bit More Encouragement . . .
www.feelfreetoprosper.com/sam

Okay . . . I think I got my message across. ☺

Follow-Up to Lesson One

I hope this finds you well and adjusting to your new conscious-ness—you know—the one completely devoid of all negative words and thoughts (well, okay . . . words) about your finances. If you are with the program, then you should feel just a little lighter and lighter as time goes by. It's amazing how eliminating the words that are not representative of who we truly are can affect the way we feel. And we are creating a vacuum of sorts, a space that can now be filled with life-giving, life-enhancing, abundance-producing words and thoughts that will receive no opposition and manifest results according to our heartfelt desires. We are getting ready for the fun stuff.

Following is a question that many new students may have on their minds, and I have provided a helpful answer. Remember that although the principles I teach apply to everyone at every level of consciousness, students are at various levels of prosperity con-sciousness and learning. Even if this particular question does not apply to your situation, the answer and the process will, so adapt and apply the answer to your own level of prosperity and to any area that you are working on.

Question

How does one stop those "I can't" or "I don't have" thoughts regarding money for our day-to-day living expenses, when the appearance is that we just don't have enough?

It is **very important** that you stop those negative ("I can't") thoughts as soon as they arise. That's why I gave you the "Wealth, Success" words for the first lesson period, because it's a shortcut to stop those thoughts without having to remember or repeat a longer affirmation. Remember the drop-by-drop in the bucket? Every time you do that you will be adding another drop, and at some point your mind is going to get the message and those negative thoughts will come less and less. But you have to tame the lion. As soon as you are aware of the negative thought, **stop**, and repeat the positive words. You may even feel that you are lying to yourself at first, and that's okay, because you will be "lying" until the "lies" become the truth. You and you alone are deciding what is true about yourself. From now on, "I can't" is not the truth. "Wealth and Success" is the truth about you.

The following will help you with this situation. So try doing this now: When the thought comes into your mind, "I can't pay . . ." immediately reverse it and say, "I can pay that bill now . . ."; "I *do* have the money for . . ."; "The way is opening up for me to pay for . . ."

Yes, you can pay the bill, you do have the money, and the way is opening up for you. If you will accept (pretend) this in your mind and feel that it is so, the money will come—somehow, in some form—through expected or unexpected channels. Say these positive phrases and relax about it . . . you have the money, so there is nothing to fear. The money is there for you and if you will do these things, it will present itself to you.

You continue with the above words and thoughts and know and feel that the money is on its way now. You do not allow fear to enter. Keep your stand. If you keep your thoughts on the goal, no matter what comes up, that goal will arrive. Call your creditor and tell them you are waiting for some money to arrive and ask them for an extension. And know that the money is going to come and your needs will be met.

The affirmations that I am giving you in this first lesson— that I'm instructing you to write twenty-five times per day . . . do it. When you do this, you may also say the affirmations aloud as you write them. This is very powerful conditioning for your subconscious "lion." These thoughts will sink into your subconscious. Give it time. It will happen.

Every time you have that negative thought, it reinforces— whether you believe it's about a big thing or a little thing. Sometimes the "casual" thoughts drop into the subconscious mind just as easily as the focused ones, because we are relaxed and not monitoring ourselves to catch them.

All of the good that you want in your life ("good" meaning money, success, jobs, happiness, health, creativity, relationships, anything you desire) is already there for you, and the Universe is ready to give it to you. But it cannot get through to you if you deny it—and that is what you are doing when you use those negatives. You are, in essence, saying to the Universe, "No, thank you." Now, that is really something to think about!

Unexpected Invitations, Gifts, Savings

Do not be surprised if, while you are applying these lessons, people invite you to dinner or events—their treat! Or you receive other complimentary invitations. Even expense-paid trips! Or you find something you wanted to buy at a great discount. Consider any happenings like these as an indication that your prosperity consciousness is starting to grow and the principles are taking effect.

As you build your prosperity consciousness, gifts from the Universe come in many forms, even winnings. Let me give you just one example of the many delightful surprises that have happened to me.

A new natural foods market was opening nearby and I received a flyer in the mail. It advertised their grand opening and mentioned drawings for several giveaways—including yoga classes, a Santa Barbara retreat, and a luxury hotel getaway. Well, I immediately thought about that hotel getaway because a friend of mine was coming to visit from the East Coast. I made a special trip to the store and when I got there, the container holding the customers' entry forms was full and there were no blank entry forms in sight.

I went to the store manager and asked for one. She handed me a pad of entry forms, I filled one out with my information and dropped it in the box. Then I released it from my mind. (We learn more about the principle of release in a later lesson.) The day I went to the store was about a week after the grand opening, and thousands of customers had already entered the drawing.

A few days later I received a telephone call from the store. You guessed it—I won that hotel getaway: luxury hotel in Santa Monica, deluxe ocean-view suite with balcony for two days (anytime/no restrictions), and dinner for two in the hotel restaurant—value about $800. Please understand that the value of the winnings was not nearly as exciting as witnessing the working of the laws and the fact that I had manifested specifically what I wanted.

New Affirmation for Lesson One

If you have been following instructions and writing the previous affirmation every day twenty-five times, that's enough. You can stop writing that affirmation now—unless you have become attached to it and it conjures up all those prosperous feelings, in which case you may continue if it feels right to you. Or you can now start writing this new affirmation. It's not as long as the previous one, but it's still filled with the truth about you **now**. Again, even though you are not learning about affirmations yet, the two that I have specifically composed for you are creating those subtle shifts in consciousness and preparing you for the deeper study. Here is your new affirmation:

I accept prosperity as my divine right.

Prosperity *is* your divine right. You have a right to prosperity and to all of the abundance of the Universe, just like you have the right to breathe the air on this planet. You never doubt your next breath, do you? When you no longer doubt your prosperity in that same way, you will be surrounded by it. That's what all of these techniques are for—removing fear and doubt and replacing them with faith and security.

That feels so good when I say this affirmation—it always lifts me out of the "doubt" state. I am counting on it doing the same for you. Write it twenty-five times every day.

Keep prospering with the new affirmation. Are you keeping notes or a journal to list the happenings you are grateful for each day?

Marilyn's Moolah Magnetizer . . .

Sitting comfortably or lying down, close your eyes, take a deep breath, and relax. You are in your own body, looking out at the world as you normally do, only your eyes are closed. Suddenly you notice that there are currency bills (the colorful bills of your own country)—$20 bills, $100 bills, $1,000 bills, whatever denominations you can imagine. They are floating toward you from above and all around. It's raining thousands of these colorful bills. They are surrounding you. They are landing in piles all around you. You extend your hands, open your palms, and let all of these bills just land wherever they want. They are drawn to you just like you are a magnet. But they are flowing gently toward you, almost in a loving way. The bills feel welcome, like they are being invited to surround you. You are inviting them into your life and you gratefully receive them because you know you deserve them. You have made a definite decision. You are now allowing the Universe to shower you with its monetary gifts. You are so grateful for this amazing shower of affection from the Universe. The Universe has always loved you and wanted you to have these gifts, but you were not open to receive them. Now you are open to receive and gladly accept your abundance. You repeat lovingly to yourself:

I am receiving, I am receiving now. I am receiving all of the wealth that the Universe has for me now.

Note: As I noted in Chapter 10, some people cannot visualize in mental pictures. There is nothing wrong with this—it's just the way their brains function. But they can visualize by "feeling" the reality of the goal they wish to attain, and still experience results.

Part 3

You began your prosperity journey by applying Lesson One and the Follow-Up to Lesson One for one week, as instructed. It's now time to listen to the recorded group mentoring session. For even greater benefit, I am including in the book important teaching highlights from the session. Part 3 includes:

- Downloadable Recording of the Group Mentoring Session

- Highlights of the Group Mentoring Session

- Prosperity Meditation

You now have the opportunity to listen to the two-hour recorded session and experience my teachings more fully as I interact with my students. You will feel like you are attending the live call.

Downloadable Recording of the
Group Mentoring Session

Now sit back, relax and listen to the recording here . . .

Group Mentoring Session*
www.feelfreetoprosper.com/session-one-audio

Please do not read the following sections—Highlights of the Group Mentoring Session or the Prosperity Meditation—until *after* you have listened to the audio recording. You can then refer to the Highlights at any time for review and reinforcement. You will find a few items that also appeared earlier in the book, but I want you to receive the full contents of this traditional lesson material. The repetition and reinforcement can only serve to benefit you.

The Prosperity Meditation that I shared in the group session is a treasured collector's item that I've included for you. I recommend you use it as often as you would like.

After listening to the audio session and reviewing the session highlights, **continue to apply the homework from Lesson One and the Follow-Up to Lesson One for <u>another full week</u>** or a bit longer. This week you may write either affirmation or you may alternate them if you prefer.

Please note that we apply the Feel Free to Prosper lessons for at least two weeks to begin creating a new pathway in the brain. After the two weeks of Lesson One, you have the option of moving

---

* The downloadable recording of the group mentoring session expires on January 1, 2026.

forward with the complete Feel Free to Prosper program, highly discounted for the readers of this book as presented below after the Prosperity Meditation. Remember, for some students it may take longer than two weeks to experience the exhilaration of results.

Highlights of the Group Mentoring Session

1. Growth and Expansion

I believe you resonated to me and to my teaching for a reason. Life is always evolving upward and onward and seeks to grow and expand. When we plant a seed in the soil, all of the power of the Universe works in and through that seed to expand it into a plant or flower. Your soul is pushing you to expand and grow and you gravitated to me because it knows that I have knowledge and answers to help you.

Think of the vast ocean of the Universe. You are not the whole ocean but you are a drop in the ocean and all of the characteristics, abilities, potential, and creative power of the ocean are in you. You cannot be separated from the ocean. You are always connected to your source.

But somewhere along your path you came to believe that there is a separation, that you are not connected to your source of good. This is an illusion that was created from the negative beliefs instilled in your mind by others, even from a very young age.

This was not your fault. This does not mean that you are undeserving, that you are doing something wrong (at least consciously), or that you are not a good person. You just acquired false beliefs and took on the beliefs of others who were unaware, and made them your own.

2. Princesses and Princes, Queens and Kings

In the wonderful 1999 film *The Cider House Rules*, Michael Caine played a doctor in a boys' orphanage. He would put his young charges to bed with these famous lines: "Goodnight, you princes of Maine, you kings of New England."* He saw the wonderful potential and perfection in these orphans.

In a sense, I feel the same about my students. Although you may feel orphaned or separated from your Source, the fact is that you are never separated and each of you is a prince or princess of prosperity and a king or queen of your consciousness. You are the son or daughter of a rich Father—the Universe, God, Divine Presence, Infinite Intelligence, Spiritual Substance, Field of All Possibilities—you are here to learn who and what you really are.

Speaking of rich children . . . if you are a parent, I want you to know that the greatest gift you can give your children is the gift of a prosperity consciousness. How would you feel knowing your children will grow up to be happy, successful adults without financial issues? This is the legacy you will give them by cultivating your own prosperity consciousness.

3. Results

You are beginning to discover your true identity. Although you are most likely concerned with manifestations relating to business and financial matters, as you continue, you are going to find that you will experience prosperity for the soul as well. You'll receive

---

* Gladstein, R. (producer) and Hallström, L. (director), *The Cider House Rules* (1999). United States: Miramax.

universal gifts relating to family and friendship and travel. Also, don't be surprised if there are manifestations of physical healing. We have had several of them in our groups.

Perhaps this is just the beginning of your journey to overcome a lack consciousness. Please remember that we are all different when it comes to background, mindset, and level of prosperity consciousness. But when it comes to the laws, it is a level playing field. We are all made of the same mind stuff. The universal laws will work for everyone in the same way the law of gravity works for all. Some will get results sooner, some later. But the results *are* coming. The Universe is listening. Remember, prosperity is your divine right.

4. Perseverance

How long does this process take?

The great New Thought teacher Catherine Ponder says that there are three stages to manifesting, and I will explain them.

Stage One is when we do our mental work—our "homework"— and we plant our seeds.

Stage Two is often a quiet time when it appears that nothing is happening, but in reality that is when everything is happening. This is the germination period. The seeds are planted and under the ground, all of the forces of nature and the Universe are coming into play to create that plant or flower or tree. But we see nothing on the surface.

Stage Three is when we reap the harvest—when our desires are fulfilled. The unfortunate thing is that most people quit and give up in the second stage because they don't see anything happening and they don't think the process is working.

Do not make that mistake. Stay with it! It takes a certain amount of time to create a new neural pathway in the brain. You may be overcoming a lifetime of acquired beliefs.

5. Core Beliefs About Your Relationship to Money

I'm going to ask you to take a few moments and quietly contemplate and determine your core belief about your relationship to money and prosperity—the overall belief you had before beginning the prosperity lessons. This belief may have been acquired in your childhood or at some later time. Do that now. Take your time.

The answers shared in my groups are usually quite common, but on occasion there are really surprising ones. Here are some of the actual core beliefs that students have shared:

- There is never enough, there will never be enough.

- Money is for somebody else, but not meant for me.

- It won't work for me, just for others.

- I don't measure up.

- I've already had my share.

- I grew up believing it was wrong to have more than others.

- It's out of reach, always around the corner.

- I have to struggle to get money.

- I have to work really hard to get money.

- I won't be able to manage it if I had money.

- I feel guilty receiving money without hard work.

- Money is not spiritual—I can't be rich and spiritual.

- My religious background taught me that money is evil.

- I can't be Christian and wealthy.

- You can't take it with you, so why have more than you need?

- I feel guilty having money and wanting more, when others have so little.

- Country songs taught us there's pride in poverty.

- I was raised to believe a "white knight" will come along and take care of me.

- My family will come knocking at my door if I have money.

Now let's look at one on the positive side . . .

One of my students came from Cuba to the United States with her family in the sixties and they literally had nothing except the clothes they wore when they arrived. At the time, the Cuban government would not let them take anything out of the country, so they had to start from scratch. And yet, she told us, she was raised to believe that if you did what was right, were a good person, and had honor, then you would always be provided for and things would always work out financially.

I find it significant—perhaps ironic—that a prosperity consciousness will often take root when one *hits bottom*, so to speak. When we are stripped of all outer means and stand naked before the Universe, we realize that there is really nowhere to go but up, and I think that is when many people will reach for the universal life jacket to pull them up and out. That is exactly what happened to me at certain times in my life. Those are the experiences that taught me the most about the laws—what worked and what didn't.

Do you feel a little better knowing that you're not alone—that others share many of these same core beliefs or even more unusual ones?

All of the negative core beliefs having to do with prosperity are the result of thoughts and ideas that are established in your subconscious mind. They are not the truth about you. This program is revealing the truth to you and will create new thought patterns to overcome the old ones. Everything will change once you understand that money is no different than the air we breathe—pure energy, pure spiritual substance—there for the asking, if you will just inhale. You are learning to inhale.

Please add this to your homework following this exercise:

You have acknowledged and expressed your core belief and that is now the end of it. Say goodbye to that negative belief. It no longer exists as the truth about you. I want you to remember this brilliant quote from Albert Einstein:

> *No problem can be solved from the same level of consciousness that created it.*

You are a prosperity student now and you prosper in every area of life, and that prosperity now includes money. I am giving you the tools that will take you there.

6. Your Habitual Words and Phrases

You are becoming increasingly aware of the impact that your words have on your life circumstances. Become aware of negative words that do not represent what you want to happen in your life. Watch for these words and expressions that may be blocking your channels to prosperity.

Think of yourself as a scientist in a laboratory of the mind. You are brewing a new consciousness. This means there must be no contaminants—from you or from others, especially while you are creating this shift.

Therefore you will watch for and eliminate from your vocabulary certain words that do not represent what you want—words like "struggle," "stressed," "afraid," "hard," "tough," "worried." These are hidden words that you may often use without realizing it—it is just a habit. But it keeps you where you don't want to be.

You must now create new habits of speech. Remember that the subconscious mind hears everything and accepts our words as an order. Become creative in the way you phrase your sentences and respond to others. There are many ways to make a point—learn to choose a positive phrase.

Let me give you some examples:

1. How can you negotiate a price for services without saying or thinking, "I can't afford . . . "?

It's pretty simple, really. It is not necessary to come from a mindset of lack when your goal is to stay within your budget. You can instead speak like a practical businessperson who knows what he/she wants:

I would love to do business with you (or use your service), but I would need to have a better price.

I appreciate your value, but I would require a better price.

Can you give me a better price to accommodate my current budget?

I believe we could work together if you are able to lower your price and still be compensated adequately.

Big difference, isn't it?

2. You are asked to donate to a charity. You would like to contribute but don't have the funds at this time. Most people would say . . .

I'm sorry, I would like to, but I just don't have the money (or can't afford it) right now. (Some people use this as an excuse even if they **have** the money but don't wish to donate.)

You can respond in this way:

If you would please call me back in the future, I would love to contribute then.

3. There is something you want to buy. You tell yourself:

I can't afford that. I don't have enough money.

Instead:

I deserve to have that. I am waiting for money to arrive and soon I will buy it.

I don't care if you are referring to a new blouse or a new Mercedes. The law will work for anything in life.

So, which of the phrases given represents what you want your subconscious mind to accept as an order? Which of the phrases represents where you want to be in life?

Remember what I say: If you don't want it, don't say it. That goes for written words also . . . written words are especially powerful, as you are already discovering in your lesson work.

7. Source vs. Channels

I am going to share with you one of the most important components of my teachings.

If you will grasp this, it will change your financial life. And it can change your entire life if you broaden your understanding beyond the monetary aspect. So listen carefully.

Your business is not your source of income. Your business, job, clients, sales, investments, spouse—none of these are your source of income. There is only one source of income—the Universe, God, Divine Presence, Formless Substance, Quantum Field (whatever your concept is of that universal source of good). The Universe is your source of supply.

That is the only source of your supply. All of those other avenues are **channels** for your supply. But they are not the source of your supply. When you truly understand and know this, then you will open the pipeline to the unlimited channels of supply that exist for you. And there are unlimited channels through which your good can come to you, the unexpected along with the expected. But you can only become open and receptive to these free-flowing channels when you put your complete reliance on the true source.

Let's use the analogy of a kitchen faucet. The faucet is not the source of water. It's only a channel. If that channel is broken or closed, then there are an infinite number of other channels through which we can get our water. So when we "loosen up" our dependency or reliance on any particular channel for our supply and rely only on our Source—then all channels will open for our good to flow to us. And the more **speedily** will our good flow.

When you look to your true Source of supply, it will become the Senior Partner in your business and your life and you will prosper. You will be in your right place with the right people. You will be at peace. Obviously, there are other lessons you are learning to speed your journey on the path to prosperity, but I cannot emphasize enough the importance of this one.

The more you acknowledge the Source for every blessing and result that comes to you, the more they will keep increasing. Sometimes in the early stages of doing this work, one will wonder if it would have happened anyway. Don't rationalize it away. Just accept that the laws are working for you and assume they are the reason for your results. By acknowledging and thanking the Universe, you maintain a state of consciousness that attracts even more.

8. Apparent Setbacks While Doing This Work

If you happen to experience an apparent setback while doing your prosperity work, you will be relieved to know that this is the aftermath (the effect) of previous lack thoughts and beliefs (the cause). It's important to calmly "weather the storm" and ride with it. All of the new thoughts and ideas that you are instilling in your mind will soon result in new circumstances and conditions. So do not be alarmed by this and don't give up! Keep planting new seeds, and flowers will replace the weeds. We live in a time/space world and a certain amount of time elapses between a cause and its effect. So even if you temporarily experience the effects of the old way of thinking, you'll soon be experiencing the effects of the new.

9. Keeping the Silence

We should not announce our pending manifestations to others. It's wise to keep silent about your results and goals until they are consummated. Manifestations can be very exciting and you may want to share as soon as they begin, but don't announce them until they are completed. This keeps the creative energy focused like a laser, maintains your clear connection with the Universe during the completion stages, and keeps your reliance on your Source. So wait until completion, until contracts are signed or agreements confirmed—until you have a "done deal." This also prevents us from being influenced by the unconscious agendas of others.

10. Do I Accept Everything the Universe Brings?

You do not have to accept every opportunity that presents itself while applying these teachings. Follow your intuition, listen to your feelings, and pay attention to your body symptoms. I believe that sometimes options arrive so that you know you have a choice or so that you can make a clearer decision about what you really want. I also believe that the right decision always feels peaceful.

When we step out in faith to release the lesser, the greater will appear. Why settle for less than we really want?

Also, as mentioned earlier, sometimes you may attract situations that are the effect from an earlier cause. Be happy in knowing that the lessons you are applying now are creating new causes that will result in new effects—the ones you really want.

11. Fast Walking, Cardio Exercise

I am going to give you another assignment, which not only will speed your progress with the lessons, but also will enhance your physical condition and mental well-being.

Unless there is a physical reason you cannot do so, I would like you to put on your comfortable athletic shoes and go outdoors and walk fast. A brisk pace will increase your heart rate and your brain will produce endorphins—those feel-good hormones that make life and the world look rosy. While walking fast, do your mental homework. Repeat "wealth, success" or say affirmations to the rhythm of your steps. I believe that the words will drop easily into the subconscious during this heightened endorphin state.

Of course, other forms of cardio/aerobic exercise are just as good as long as they get your heart rate up and endorphins flowing. I find walking easy for most people and it provides rhythm for the mental exercises.

12. Have Fun with Prosperity—Lighten Up!

We must learn to have fun with prosperity. A joyous state attracts prosperity. If you have fun with prosperity, you will magnetize it. In some of my group programs, I've had the entire group of students "sound off" with Prosperity Boot Camp Drills for fun. The subconscious mind loves rhythm and rhyme, so these artfully worded drills could be very effective. Many students listening to the recording said their children were having fun running around the house repeating the drills.

Can you stay in a negative state while doing these? No way. And even if it feels silly, I say we can feel silly all the way to the bank.

13. Continue with Lesson One

Continue to apply Lesson One. This second week can be very significant. Anything can happen now! As many students have said, "What a ride!"

14. Prosperity Meditation

Included with your program is a wonderful Prosperity Meditation I found decades ago that is no longer in print and that I consider a collector's item. United Centers for Spiritual Living has graciously granted me permission to use it. My students love this meditation. Feel free to use it lovingly morning or night or both.

Prosperity Meditation

Today I consciously share in the gifts of life. I open my whole thought and my whole being to the divine influence. I empty myself of everything that denies the good I desire and I establish my mind in positive expectancy, knowing that all the good there is belongs to anyone who will take it. I receive the divine gift right now. I enter right now into my spiritual inheritance. Today I am richly blessed as the gifts of life flow to me from every source.

The Universal substance is supplying me now with everything I need. Good comes freely to me, and only good goes out from me. I accept abundance. Everything I have increases. I identify with success. Whatever I need—whenever I need it, wherever I need it, for as long as I need it—is always at hand.

Spirit prospers everything I do, increases every good I possess, and brings success and abundance into my life. Everything I think about and do is animated by the divine Presence, sustained by the universal Power, and multiplied by infinite Goodness. Recognizing Spirit as the center and source of all that exists, I consciously unite with it, proclaiming its presence and activity in all my affairs. Every desire of my heart is now fulfilled, and I am bountifully prospered in all that I do.*

* Reprinted with permission from World Ministry of Prayer: a program of Centers for Spiritual Living, *Prosperity* pamphlet.

The Feel Free to Prosper Audio Program

After applying the lessons in this book, if your heart is prompting you to continue with the Feel Free to Prosper lessons and teachings, all six lessons and all eight recorded sessions are included in my flagship self-study Feel Free to Prosper® Audio Program.

As a reader of this book and beginning Feel Free to Prosper student, with proof of your book purchase, you are entitled to purchase the complete program for a highly discounted price. You can find all the details here:

The Feel Free to Prosper Audio Program
www.feelfreetoprosper.com/readers

There seem to be many paths, but the quickest, most complete and permanent path to prosperity is recognition of the Divinity within you. You are a spark of the Divine. Know it.

—MARILYN

Acknowledgments

My deepest gratitude goes to my dear friends Michael Rodriguez, Susan Moel, and Kathleen Jaap. They have always given me their unconditional love and support, and believed in me when I didn't believe in myself.

Paul S. Levine, my original agent, encouraged me to finish my memoir and was tenacious in getting me to write a proposal for this book. Writer Karen Gordon created a fantastic proposal before I added my material to complete it. An added gift is her friendship and support. Publisher Marc Allen at New World Library provided inspiration and was an early influence in the evolution of this book. Independent consultant Claudia Suzanne offered technical expertise and friendship. Bill Gladstone, my agent, arrived by divine appointment to bring the book to fruition. My publisher, Joel Fotinos at Penguin Random House, was destined to fulfill my mission as he stepped out in faith to take me on. Andrew Yackira, my editor at Penguin, honored my words and voice as we polished the dream. The talents of the production team, copy editors, managing editorial, and designers brought the dream to life.

Adrian Scott is the founder of Ryze, the former social networking site that provided the launching platform for my Feel Free to Prosper teachings and programs. Had it not been for the Ryze community and the members who became my students and my audience, I would not have expressed my teachings in writing or created my memoir, which ultimately resulted in my books.

Loving gratitude to Rev. June Haskell, whose words, "You can teach, you know," took root in the soil of my subconscious and changed my life forever.

My web consultants, Russ Jackman, Susan McCool, and Carma Spence, gave me their loyalty and the technical support needed to free my mind. Dianne Reum is the wonderful artist who created my adorable aliens, a special treasure.

Most of all, I want to acknowledge the Universal Presence from which all manifestations flow and express my deepest gratitude for all of its blessings, including those that are listed above as well as those that are still to come.

About the Author

Marilyn Jenett is a renowned prosperity mentor with an international following. She is also an accomplished entrepreneur. Her former business, Marilyn Jenett Locations, attracted the world's largest corporate clients and major media publicity for over twenty years.

Marilyn's achievements in the business world were the result of applying her prosperity principles—with the "Universe as her marketing department."

In 2003, she founded the Feel Free to Prosper® program to mentor and teach others to become aligned with the universal laws and accept their right to prosper. Thousands have applied her simple yet powerful techniques based on mental and spiritual laws to manifest striking results and learn how to put the "Universe on speed dial."

Decades ago, Marilyn devoted herself to the study of manifestation laws and prosperity principles. She buried herself in the teachings and literature of the legendary, brilliant masters of mental and spiritual science. She was privileged to study with some of the original legends in the field—she even met with Dr. Joseph Murphy in his home, just minutes away. She now continues the legacy with her own teachings, unique style, and proprietary techniques.

Her victory in overcoming her own "lack" consciousness culminated in her faith and conviction in the laws and recognition of her life's purpose—and spiritual obligation—to teach others. Marilyn intuitively sought a method that would allow others to quickly and easily grasp and understand these laws, without having to go through a long journey similar to hers. She was convinced simplicity was the key.

Marilyn's fascinating memoir, *Feel Free to Prosper: An Entrepreneurial Memoir of Synchronicity and Guidance*—written entirely online—attracted extraordinary public attention and ultimately led to literary agents and publishing offers based on her teachings. She knows that this honor confirms that she is following her destined path.

It is Marilyn's deepest desire that this book will provide the inspiration and the tools for the reader to become aware of and connect with his or her own source of synchronicity and guidance—and finally feel free to prosper.

Image Credits

Billboard image: Copyright © Marilyn Jenett

Billboard and butterfly photos: Sailorman/Dreamstime.com

Billboard design: Sean Taylor

Cartoons: Dianne L. Reum

Digital devices clip art: Alexmillos/Dreamstime.com

"Forget the How" graphic: DebiPayneDesigns.com